Best of Fons&Porter®

patriotic Quilts

FONS & PORTER STAFF
Editors-in-Chief Marianne Fons and Liz Porter

Editor Jean Nolte
Assistant Editor Diane Tomlinson
Managing Editor Debra Finan
Technical Writer Kristine Peterson

Art Director Tony Jacobson

Editorial Assistant Mandy Couture
Sewing Specialist Cindy Hathaway

Contributing Photographers Dean Tanner, Katie Downey, Craig Anderson
Contributing Photo Assistant DeElda Wittmack

Publisher Kristi Loeffelholz
Advertising Manager Cristy Adamski
Retail Manager Sharon Hart
Web Site Manager Phillip Zacharias
Customer Service Manager Tiffiny Bond
Fons & Porter Staff Peggy Garner, Shelle Goodwin, Kimberly Romero,
Laura Saner, Karol Skeffington, Yvonne Smith, Anne Welker, Karla Wesselmann

New Track Media LLC
President and CEO Stephen J. Kent
Chief Financial Officer Mark F. Arnett
President, Book Publishing W. Budge Wallis
Vice President/Group Publisher Tina Battock
Vice President, Circulation Nicole McGuire
Vice President, Production Barbara Schmitz

Our Mission Statement
Our goal is for you to enjoy making quilts as much as we do.

LEISURE ARTS STAFF
Editor-in-Chief Susan White Sullivan
Quilt and Craft Publications Director Cheryl Johnson
Special Projects Director Susan Frantz Wiles
Senior Prepress Director Mark Hawkins
Imaging Technician Stephanie Johnson
Prepress Technician Janie Marie Wright
Publishing Systems Administrator Becky Riddle
Mac Information Technology Specialist Robert Young

President and Chief Executive Officer Rick Barton
Vice President of Sales Mike Behar
Director of Finance and Administration Laticia Mull Dittrich
National Sales Director Martha Adams
Creative Services Chaska Lucas
Information Technology Director Hermine Linz
Controller Francis Caple
Vice President, Operations Jim Dittrich
Retail Customer Service Manager Stan Raynor
Print Production Manager Fred F. Pruss

Library of Congress Control Number: 2011934657
ISBN-13/EAN: 978-1-60900-349-4

10 9 8 7 6 5 4 3 2

We're thrilled to bring you this collection of some of our very favorite patriotic quilts! The projects we've included are among our most popular of all time. You'll find challenging as well as easy patchwork, plus dashes of lovely appliqué. Enjoy the beautiful photography as you browse through the pages to find the quilt that's just right for you. Whether you prefer traditional or contemporary fabrics, you'll find plenty to love. You'll also appreciate our trademarked *Sew Easy* lessons that will guide you via step-by-step photography through any project-specific special techniques. Perhaps you'll want to make a quilt for someone who has served or is currently serving in the military. Patchwork is patriotic!

Happy quilting,

Marianne & Liz

Table of Contents

102

96

14

Techniques

24

64

52

Fringed Stars

Jeanette Pié designed this patriotic quilt that incorporates patchwork, raw edge appliqué, and good ol' red, white, and blue.

PROJECT RATING: EASY

Size: 51" × 68"

Blocks: 20 (9" × 10") Star blocks

MATERIALS

5 fat quarters★ assorted red prints for stars

5 fat quarters★ assorted blue prints for stars

½ yard each of 5 assorted beige prints for block backgrounds and sashing

1¼ yards red print for sashing

⅜ yard medium blue print for sashing squares

½ yard dark blue print for binding

3¼ yards backing fabric

Twin-size quilt batting

★fat quarter = 18" × 20"

Cutting

Measurements include ¼" seam allowances. Patterns for stars are on page 9.

From each fat quarter, cut:

• 2 Large Stars.

• 2 Medium Stars.

• 2 Small Stars.

From each beige print, cut:

• 3 (1½"-wide) strips for strip sets.

• 4 (10" × 11") background rectangles.

From red print, cut:

• 26 (1½"-wide) strips for strip sets.

From medium blue print, cut:

• 3 (3½"-wide) strips. From strips, cut 30 (3½") sashing squares.

From dark blue print, cut:

• 7 (2¼"-wide) strips for binding.

Block Assembly

1. Fold each background rectangle in half lengthwise; lightly press crease to mark center.

2. Fold each star in half lengthwise; press to mark center.

3. Position 1 large red star on 1 background rectangle, matching folds and centering star on background as shown in *Star Placement Diagrams*. Pin in place. Stitch around star ¼" inside edge. Turn block over and carefully cut away background fabric about ¼" inside stitching line.

4. In the same manner, center 1 medium blue star on red star. Stitch around blue star ¼" inside edge. Turn block over and cut away center of red star fabric.

Fold

Star Placement Diagrams

5. Center 1 small red star on medium blue star. Stitch around the red star ¼" from the edge. Turn block over and remove center of blue star fabric to complete 1 block. Make 10 red blocks.

6. Make 10 blue blocks using large blue, medium red, and small blue stars.

7. Referring to *Cutting Diagrams*, cut each block in half lengthwise and crosswise. **NOTE:** Do not move block between cuts.

Cutting Diagrams

8. Lay out 4 different quarter blocks as shown in *Block Assembly Diagrams*. Join quarters to complete 1 block. Make 20 blocks.

Block Assembly Diagrams

Sashing Assembly

1. Join 2 red print strips and 1 beige print strip as shown in *Strip Set Diagram*. Make 13 strip sets.

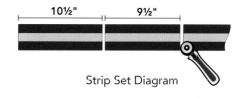

10½"   9½"

Strip Set Diagram

2. From each strip set, cut 2 (10½"-wide) and 2 (9½"-wide) sashing segments.

Quilt Assembly

1. Lay out blocks, sashing strips and sashing squares as shown in photo.

2. Join into rows; join rows to complete quilt top.

Finishing

1. Divide backing fabric into 2 (1⅝-yard) lengths. Join panels lengthwise. Seam will run horizontally.

2. Layer backing, batting, and quilt top; baste. Quilt as desired. Quilt shown was quilted in the ditch around blocks and in sashing, ¼" inside the edge of each star, and with stars in the sashing squares, wavy lines in the beige sashing, and stippling in the block backgrounds.

3. Join 2¼"-wide dark blue print strips into 1 continuous piece for straight-grain French-fold binding. Add binding to quilt.

4. Wash and dry quilt so edges of stars fray.

DESIGNER

Jeanette Pié enjoys designing quilt patterns and hosting Quilters' Getaways several times a year.

Contact her at:
Jeanette@talkingquilts.com
www.easyaspiedesigns.com

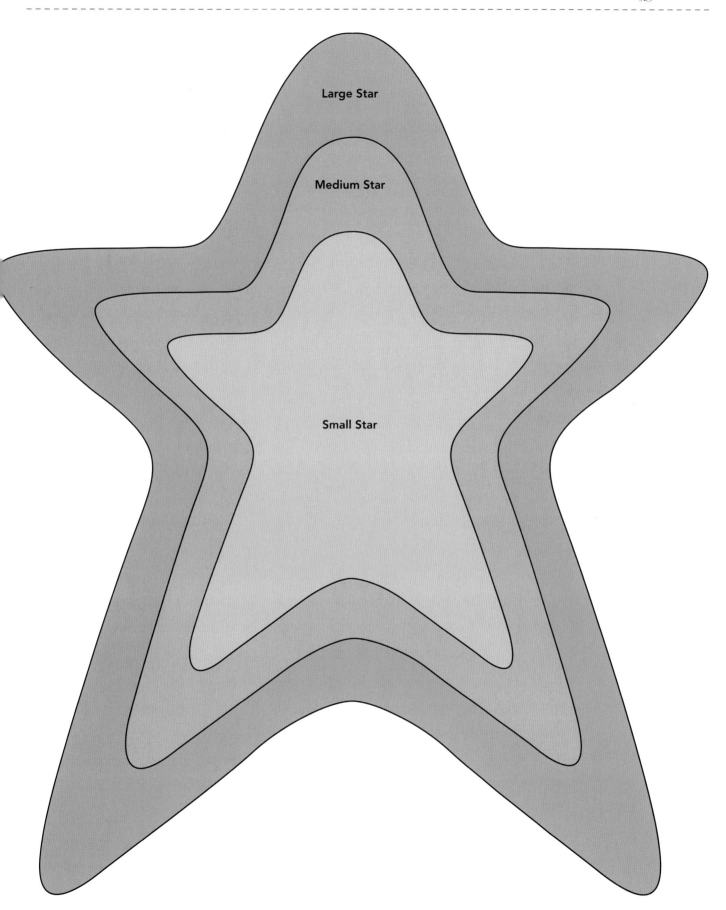

Large Star

Medium Star

Small Star

QUILT BY **Marianne Fons and Liz Porter.**

Vincent's Quilt

Marianne and Liz designed this quilt for a young sailor who served
on a submarine with Liz's son Jake.

Size: 67½" × 82½"

Blocks: 50 (7½") Star blocks

49 (7½") Stripe blocks

MATERIALS

50 (6") squares of gold or tan
fabrics for Stars

50 (8") squares of medium to dark
blue prints for Star backgrounds

2 yards red print for strip sets

1¼ yards cream print for strip sets

Paper-backed fusible web

Fine-tip permanent pen (optional)

¾ yard red stripe for binding

5 yards backing fabric

Twin-size batting

Cutting

Measurements include ¼" seam allowances. Pattern for Star is on page 12. Follow manufacturer's instructions for using fusible web. See *Sew Easy: Windowing Fusible Appliqué* on page 13.

From each gold or tan fabric, cut:

• 1 Star.

From red print, cut:

• 30 (2"-wide) strips for strip sets.

From cream print, cut:

• 20 (2"-wide) strips for strip sets.

From red stripe fabric, cut:

• 8 (2¼"-wide) strips for binding.

Star Block Assembly

1. If desired, use fine-tip permanent pen to write a message and sign each star.

2. Fuse 1 star to 1 blue square as shown in *Star Block Diagram*.

3. Blanket stitch around star to complete Star block. Make 50 Star blocks.

Star Block Diagram

Stripe Block Assembly

1. Join 3 red print strips and 2 cream strips as shown in *Strip Set Diagram*. Make 10 strip sets.

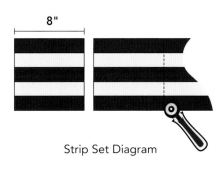

Strip Set Diagram

2. From strip sets, cut 49 (8"-wide) segments for Stripe blocks *(Stripe Block Diagram)*.

Stripe Block Diagram

Quilt Assembly

1. Join 5 Star blocks and 4 Stripe blocks as shown in *Row A Diagram*. Make 6 Row A.

2. Join 5 Stripe blocks and 4 Star blocks as shown in *Row B Diagram*. Make 5 Row B.

Sew **Smart**™

Double check direction of Stripe blocks so you don't turn one the wrong way like we did! —Marianne & Liz

3. Referring to photograph on page 10, join rows to complete quilt top.

Finishing

1. Divide backing fabric into 2 (2½-yard) lengths. Cut 1 piece in half lengthwise to make 2 narrow panels. Join 1 narrow panel to each side of wider panel; press seam allowances toward narrow panels.

2. Layer backing, batting, and quilt top; baste. Quilt as desired. Quilt shown outline quilted around stars.

Row A Diagram

Row B Diagram

Remaining areas were quilted with free-form stars and assorted patriotic phrases.

3. Join 2¼"-wide red stripe strips into 1 continuous piece for straight-grain French-fold binding. Add binding to quilt. ✳

Star

Windowing Fusible Appliqué

Choose a lightweight "sewable" fusible product. The staff at your favorite quilt shop can recommend brands. Always read and follow manufacturer's instructions for proper fusing time and iron temperature.

1. Trace appliqué motifs onto paper side of fusible web, making a separate tracing for each appliqué needed (*Photo A*).

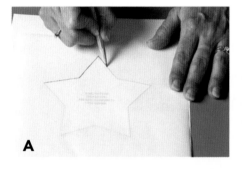

2. Roughly cut out drawn appliqué shapes, cutting about ¼" outside drawn lines (*Photo B*).

3. "Window" fusible by trimming out the interior of the shape, leaving a scant ¼" inside drawn line (*Photo C*). Follow manufacturer's instructions to fuse web side of each shape to wrong side of appliqué fabric.

4. Cut out appliqués, cutting carefully on drawn outline (*Photo D*). Only a thin band of fusible web frames the shape.

5. Peel off paper backing (*Photo E*). Position appliqué in place on background fabric, and follow manufacturer's instructions to fuse shapes in place.

Sew Smart™

If you have trouble peeling off the paper backing, try scoring paper with a pin to give you an edge to begin with. —Marianne

QUILT BY **Liz Porter**.
MACHINE QUILTED BY **Kelly Ashton**.

Homespun Galaxy

"Plaids are my favorite fabrics. I love collecting them and playing around with them until I find the perfect design," says Liz Porter. This heartwarming quilt is made completely from homespun plaids.

PROJECT RATING: INTERMEDIATE

Size: 71½" × 97"

Blocks: 8 (12") Large Star blocks
43 (6") Small Star blocks

MATERIALS

8 fat eighths★ assorted medium/
    dark plaids for large star blocks
8 fat quarters★★ assorted medium/
    dark plaids for small star blocks
4¼ yards tan plaid for background
3¼ yards red plaid for borders and
    binding
Fons & Porter Quarter Inch Seam
    Marker (optional)
6 yards backing fabric
Queen-size quilt batting
★fat eighth = 9" × 20"
★★fat quarter = 18" × 20"

Cutting

Measurements include ¼" seam allowances. Border strips are exact length needed. You may want to make them longer to allow for piecing variations.

From each fat eighth, cut:
• 1 (5¼"-wide) strip. From strip, cut 2 (5¼") A squares and 1 (4½") B square.

From each fat quarter, cut:
• 2 (3¼"-wide) strips. From strips, cut 12 (3¼") C squares.
• 1 (2½"-wide) strip. From strip, cut 6 (2½") D squares.

From tan plaid, cut:
• 8 (6½"-wide) strips. From strips, cut 24 (6½" × 12½") E rectangles.
• 3 (5¼"-wide) strips. From strips, cut 16 (5¼") A squares.
• 4 (4½"-wide) strips. From strips, cut 32 (4½") B squares.
• 8 (3¼"-wide) strips. From strips, cut 86 (3¼") C squares.

- 11 (2½"-wide) strips. From strips, cut 172 (2½") D squares.

From red plaid, cut:

- 2 (9¾"-wide) strips. From strips, cut 7 (9¾") squares. Cut squares in half diagonally in both directions to make 28 side setting triangles (2 are extra.)

- 1 (9⅜"-wide) strip. From strip, cut 2 (9⅜") squares. Cut squares in half diagonally to make 4 corner setting triangles.

- 8 (6½"-wide) strips. Piece strips to make 2 (6½" × 85½") side borders and 2 (6½" × 72") top and bottom borders.

- 9 (2¼"-wide) strips for binding.

> ## Sew **Smart**™
> To make Hourglass Units using the Fons & Porter Quarter Inch Seam Marker, see *Sew Easy: Quick Half-Square Triangle Units* on page 57.
> —Liz

Block Assembly

1. Referring to *Hourglass Unit Diagrams*, draw a diagonal line from corner to corner on wrong side of 2 tan plaid A squares. Place 1 marked square atop 1 plaid A square; right sides facing. Stitch along marked sewing lines. Repeat with other marked tan A square and matching plaid A square.

2. Cut between rows of stitching to make 4 triangle-squares. Press seam allowances toward darker fabric.

3. Draw a diagonal line from corner to corner on wrong side of 2 triangle-squares, perpendicular to seam. Then draw sewing lines on each side of the first line, ¼" away. With right sides facing, place 1 triangle-square with drawn line atop matching triangle-

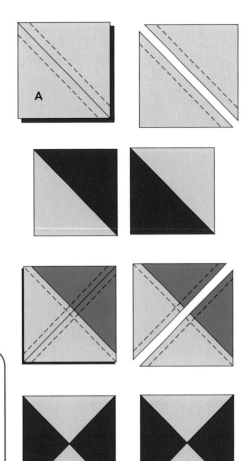

Hourglass Unit Diagrams

square, with opposite fabrics facing. Stitch along both drawn lines.

4. Cut between rows of stitching to make 4 Hourglass Units. Press seam allowances to 1 side.

5. Lay out 1 plaid B square, 4 tan B squares, and 4 Hourglass Units as shown in *Block Assembly Diagram*. Join into rows; join rows to complete 1 Large Star block. Make 8 Large Star blocks.

6. In the same manner, use 2 tan C squares and 2 plaid C squares to make 4 Hourglass Units.

7. Lay out 1 plaid D square, 4 tan D squares, and 4 Hourglass Units. Join into rows; join rows to complete 1 Small Star block. Make 43 Small Star blocks.

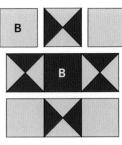

Block Assembly Diagram

Block Diagram

Quilt Assembly

1. Lay out Star blocks, tan E rectangles, and red plaid setting triangles as shown in *Quilt Top Assembly Diagram*.

2. Join into diagonal rows; join rows to complete quilt center.

3. Add red plaid side borders to quilt center. Add red plaid top and bottom borders to quilt.

Finishing

1. Divide backing fabric into 2 (3-yard) lengths. Divide 1 piece in half lengthwise to make 2 narrow panels. Join 1 narrow panel to each side of wider panel. Press seam allowances toward narrow panels.

2. Layer backing, batting, and quilt top; baste. Quilt as desired. Quilt shown was quilted with a grid in star blocks and a feather pattern in background and borders *(Quilting Diagram)*.

3. Join 2¼"-wide red plaid strips into 1 continuous piece for straight-grain French-fold binding. Add binding to quilt. ✳

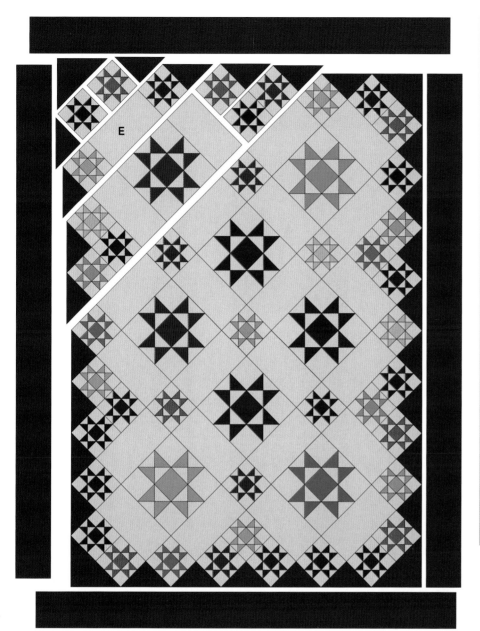

Quilt Top Assembly Diagram

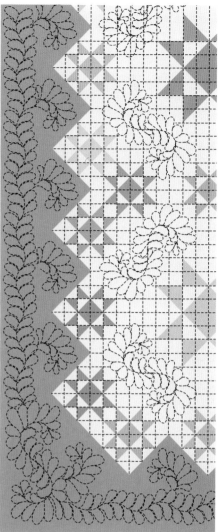

Quilting Diagram

TRIED & TRUE

Use a focus print in the center of each of your star blocks. Fabrics shown are from Northcott.

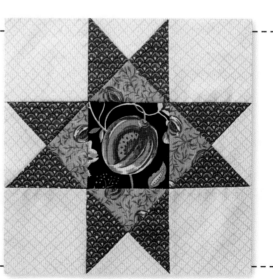

Texas Log Cabin

Marianne combined a variety of 1890s-style reproduction prints for her classic Log Cabin quilt. She arranged the blocks in a Sunshine and Shadow setting and appliquéd stars where the light shirting prints come together. Marianne explains, "I grew up in Texas, and the star shape I used on the blocks and in the border reminds me of a Texas Ranger's badge."

PROJECT RATING: INTERMEDIATE

Size: 67" × 94"

Blocks: 96 (6¾") Log Cabin blocks

MATERIALS

- 38 fat quarters★ assorted dark prints in red, blue, grey, green, pink, purple, brown, and gold
- 20 fat quarters★ assorted light prints in beige, tan, and cream
- 1 yard red solid for block centers, inner border, and binding
- 5¾ yards backing fabric
- Paper-backed fusible web
- Full-size quilt batting
- ★fat quarter = 18" × 20"

Cutting

Measurements include ¼" seam allowances. Because there are so many pieces which are similar in size, you may want to label them as you cut. Border strips are exact length needed. You may want to make them longer to allow for piecing variations. Patterns for Stars are on page 23. Follow manufacturer's instructions for using fusible web.

From dark print fat quarters, cut a total of:

- 304 (1¼"-wide) strips. From strips, cut:
  - 96 each strips #15 and #16.
  - 142 strip #12.
  - 164 each strips #11, #8, #7, #4, and #3.
  - 8 strip #1.
- 24 Large Stars.
- 30 Small Stars.

See *Cutting Chart for 1 Log Cabin Block* for strip lengths.

From light print fat quarters, cut a total of:

- 240 (1¼"-wide) strips. From strips, cut:
  - 96 strip #14.
  - 126 strip #13.
  - 156 each strips #10, #9, #6, #5, and #2.
  - 134 strip #1.

See *Cutting Chart for 1 Log Cabin Block* for strip lengths.

From red solid, cut:

- 9 (2¼"-wide) strips for binding.
- 4 (1¼"-wide) strips. From strips, cut 126 (1¼") center squares.
- 7 (⅞"-wide) strips. Piece strips to make 2 (⅞" × 81½") side inner borders and 2 (⅞" × 55¼") top and bottom inner borders.

Log Cabin Block Assembly

1. Lay out pieces as shown in *Log Cabin Block Diagram*.

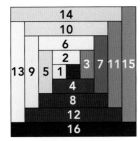

Log Cabin Block Diagram

2. Join strips in numerical order to complete 1 Log Cabin block. Make 96 Log Cabin blocks.

3. Join 4 Log Cabin blocks to make 1 Block Unit (*Block Unit Diagram*). Referring to *Quilt Top Assembly Diagram* for placement, appliqué 1 Large Star to center of Block Unit.

Cutting Chart for 1 Log Cabin Block

CUT ALL STRIPS 1¼" WIDE

Dark Strips	Light Strips	Strip Length
#16		7¼"
#15	#14	6½"
#12	#13	5¾"
#11	#10	5"
#8	#9	4¼"
#7	#6	3½"
#4	#5	2¾"
#3	#2	2"
	#1	1¼"

Block Unit Diagram

Sew **Smart**™

To avoid stiffness when appliquéing stars, window the fusible web and cut away background fabric from behind stars. See **Sew Easy: Windowing Fusible Appliqué** on page 13. —Marianne

---

Quilt Assembly

1. Lay out Block Units as shown in *Quilt Top Assembly Diagram*. Join into horizontal rows; join rows to complete quilt center.

2. Add red side inner borders to quilt center. Add top and bottom inner borders to quilt.

Log Cabin Border Assembly

1. Lay out dark and light pieces as shown in *Border Unit A Diagram*. Join strip #2 to strip #11, strip #5 to strip #8, strip #6 to strip #7, strip #9 to strip #4, strip #10 to strip #3, and strip #13 to red center. Join strips to make 1 Border Unit A. Make 30 Border Unit A. In the same manner, make 30 Border Unit B (*Border Unit B Diagram*).

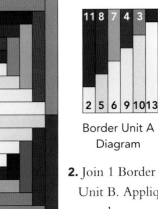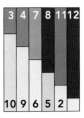

Border Unit A Diagram	Border Unit B Diagram

2. Join 1 Border Unit A and 1 Border Unit B. Appliqué 1 Small Star over seam between units. Make 30 A/B Border Units.

3. Join 1 dark strip #12 and one light square #1 to make 1 Border Unit C (*Border Unit C Diagram*). Make 8 Border Unit C.

Border Unit C Diagram

4. Lay out strips as shown in *Corner Block Diagrams*. Join pieces in numerical order to complete 1 Corner block. Make 4 Corner blocks.

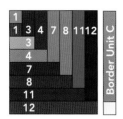

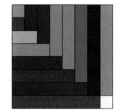

Corner Block Diagrams

5. Add one Border Unit C to each Corner Block as shown in *Corner Block Diagrams*.

6. Referring to *Quilt Top Assembly Diagram,* lay out 9 appliquéd border units and 1 Border Unit C as shown. Join to make side border. Repeat for opposite side border. Add borders to quilt.

7. Lay out 6 appliquéd border units, 1 Border Unit C, and 2 Corner blocks as shown. Join to make top border. Repeat for bottom border. Add borders to quilt.

Finishing

1. Divide backing into 2 (2⅞-yard) pieces. Cut 1 piece in half lengthwise to make 2 narrow panels. Join 1 narrow panel to each side of wider panel; press seam allowances toward narrow panels.

2. Layer backing, batting, and quilt top; baste. Quilt as desired. Quilt shown is outline quilted around stars and has

Corner Block **Border Unit C** **A/B Border Unit**

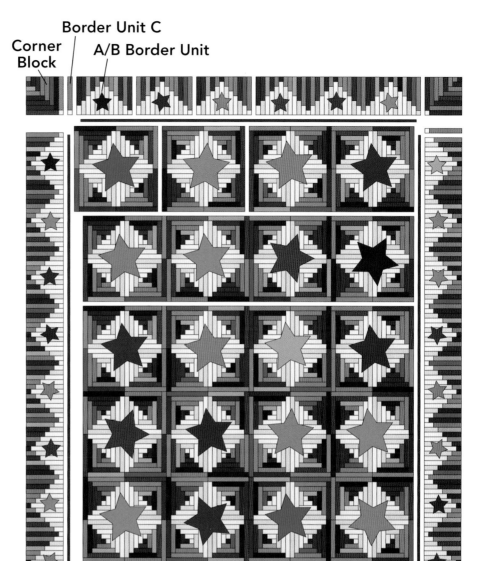

Quilt Top Assembly Diagram

star motifs in large stars, diamonds in light areas, and concentric circles in dark areas *(Quilting Diagram)*.

3. Join 2¼"-wide red strips into 1 continuous piece for straight-grain French-fold binding. Add binding to quilt.

Quilting Diagram

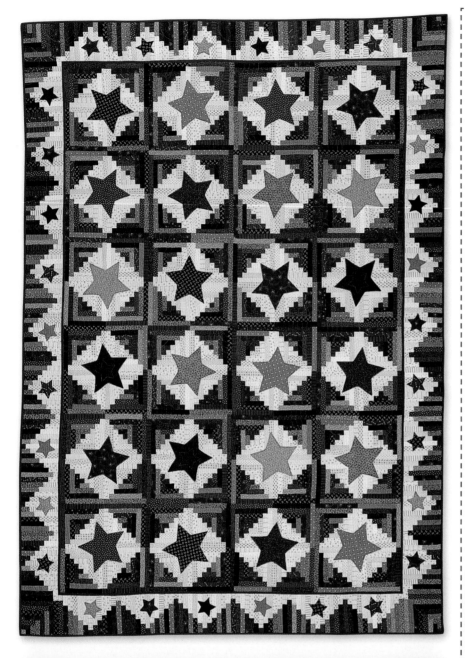

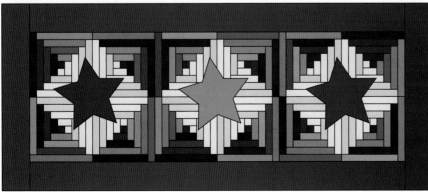

Table Runner Diagram

Texas Log Cabin Table Runner

Size: 40½" × 19½"
Blocks: 12 (6¾") Log Cabin blocks

MATERIALS

6 fat eighths★ assorted dark prints
6 fat eighths★ assorted light prints
6" square red solid
½ yard border fabric
⅜ yard binding fabric
1⅛ yards backing fabric
24" × 45" piece quilt batting
★fat eighth = 9" × 20"

Cutting

NOTE: Refer to *Cutting Chart for 1 Log Cabin Block* on page 20 to cut pieces for blocks.

From each of 3 dark prints, cut:

• 1 Large Star.
• 2 sets of dark strips.

From each of remaining 3 dark prints, cut:

• 2 sets of dark strips.

From each light print, cut:

• 2 sets of light strips.

From red solid, cut:

• 12 (1¼") center squares.

From border fabric, cut:

• 4 (3½"-wide) strips. Piece strips to make 2 (3½" × 41") top and bottom borders and 2 (3½" × 20") side borders.

From binding fabric, cut:

• 4 (2¼"-wide) strips. ✳

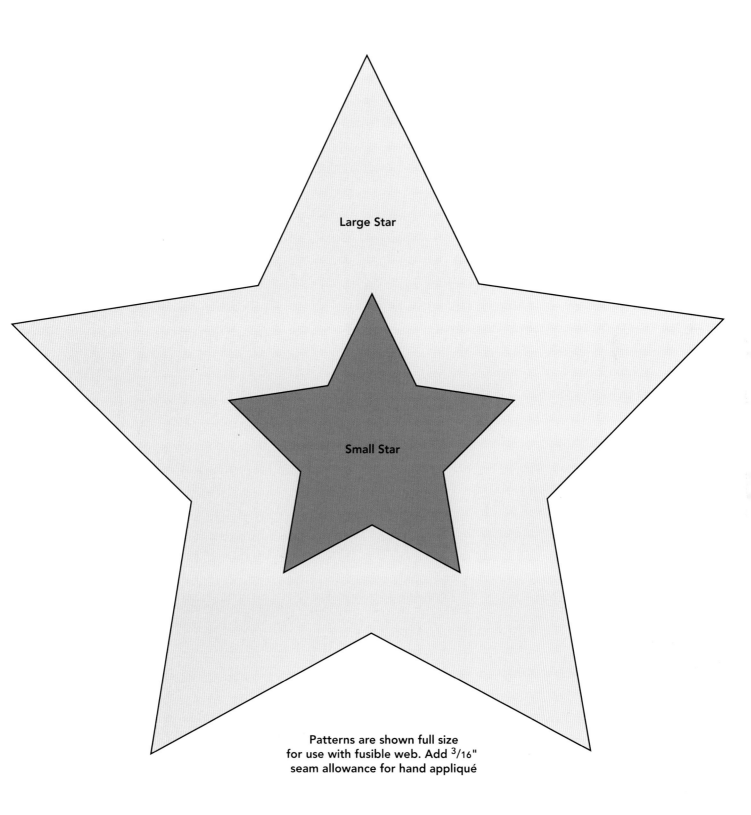

Large Star

Small Star

**Patterns are shown full size
for use with fusible web. Add ³/₁₆"
seam allowance for hand appliqué**

It's a Small Honor

Make this scrappy patriotic miniature quilt using paper foundation piecing. For a distinctive display, mount your little quilt in a picture frame as designer Diane Hansen did.

Finished Size: 4" × 6"

MATERIALS

Scraps of red, navy, green, brown, gold, and light prints
1 fat quarter★ gold print for border, binding, and backing
5" × 7" piece of flannel for batting
Paper for foundations
★fat quarter = 18" × 20"

Cutting

Measurements include ¼" seam allowances. Border strips are exact length needed. You may want to make them longer to allow for piecing variations. Foundation patterns are on page 26.

From gold print, cut:

• 2 (1"-wide) strips. From strips, cut 2 (1" × 6½") side borders and 2 (1" × 3½") top and bottom borders.
• 2 (1¾"-wide) strips for binding.
• 1 (5" × 7") rectangle for backing.

From scraps, cut:

• Pieces as needed for foundation piecing. Cut pieces at least ½" larger than the section to be covered.

Foundation Piecing

1. Trace or photocopy foundation patterns for Flag Unit, Units A and B, and Star Units 1, 2, and 3 on page 26.

2. Referring to *Sew Easy: Paper Foundation Piecing* on page 27 and *Quilt Top Assembly Diagrams,* foundation piece units in numerical order.

Star Assembly

1. Lay out Star Units as shown in *Star Assembly Diagrams.*

2. Join Star Units to complete Star.

Quilt Assembly

1. Lay out Star, Flag Unit, and A and B Units as shown in *Quilt Top Assembly Diagrams* on page 26. Join into sections. Join sections to complete quilt center.

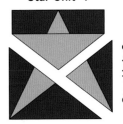

Star Unit 1

Star Unit 2

Star Unit 3

Star Assembly Diagrams

2. Add gold borders to top and bottom of quilt. Add gold borders to sides of quilt.

Finishing

1. Layer backing, flannel, and quilt top; baste. Quilt shown was not quilted because of its small size.

Unit A

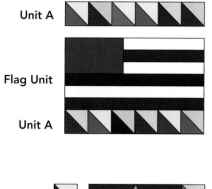

Flag Unit

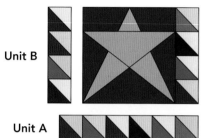

Unit A

Unit B

Unit A

Quilt Top Assembly Diagrams

Star Unit 1

Star Unit 2

Star Unit 3

2. Join 1¾"-wide gold print strips into 1 continuous piece for straight-grain French-fold binding. Add binding to quilt.

3. Quilt shown was mounted on a fabric-covered board and set in an 8" × 10" frame.

DESIGNER

Diane Hansen is a fourth-generation quilter who enjoys making patriotic scrap quilts. She has combined these two loves by designing a line of patterns for patriotic wallhangings. ✳

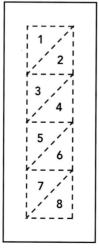

Unit B

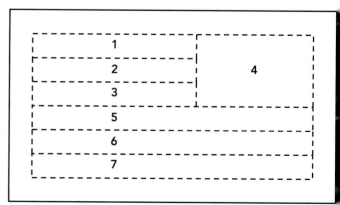

Flag Unit

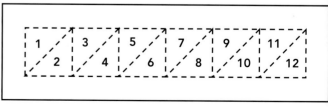

Unit A

Paper Foundation Piecing

Paper Foundation piecing is ideal for designs with odd angles and small pieces.

1. Using ruler and pencil, trace all lines and outer edge of foundation pattern onto tracing paper. Number pieces to indicate stitching order.

Sew Smart™

Save time by making photocopies on special foundation papers. Check photocopied patterns to be sure they are correct size. (Some copiers may distort copy size.) —Liz

2. Using fabric pieces that are larger than the numbered areas, place fabrics for #1 and #2 right sides together. Position paper pattern atop fabrics with printed side of paper facing you (Photo A). Make sure the fabric for #1 is under that area and that edges of fabrics extend ¼" beyond stitching line between the two sections.

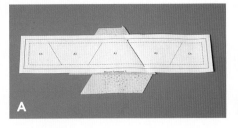

3. Using a short machine stitch so papers will tear off easily later, stitch on line between the two areas, extending stitching into seam allowances at ends of seams.

4. Open out pieces and press or finger press the seam (Photo B). The right sides of the fabric pieces will be facing out on the back side of the paper pattern.

5. Flip the work over and fold back paper pattern on stitched line. Trim seam allowance to ¼", being careful not to cut paper pattern (Photo C).

6. Continue to add pieces in numerical order until pattern is covered. Use rotary cutter and ruler to trim excess paper and fabric along outer pattern lines (Photo D).

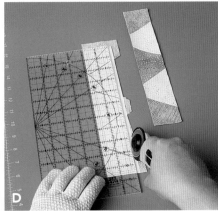

7. Carefully tear off foundation paper after blocks are joined.

Red Sky at Night

A scrappy mix of cheerful red fabrics makes a graphic statement in this eye-catching quilt.

PROJECT RATING: INTERMEDIATE

Size: 60" × 60"

Blocks: 64 (7½") Birds in the Air blocks

MATERIALS

8 fat quarters★ assorted red prints

6 fat quarters★ assorted dark prints in green, black, and blue

12 fat quarters★ assorted light prints in green, red, blue, and gray

⅝ yard red print for binding

3¾ yards backing fabric

Twin-size quilt batting

★fat quarter = 18" × 20"

Cutting

Measurements include ¼" seam allowances.

From each red print fat quarter, cut:

• 4 (8⅜") squares. Cut squares in half diagonally to make 8 half-square B triangles.

From each dark print fat quarter, cut:

• 4 (3⅜"-wide) strips. From strips, cut 17 (3⅜") squares. Cut squares in half diagonally to make 34 half-square A triangles (you will have a few extra).

From each light print fat quarter, cut:

• 4 (3⅜"-wide) strips. From strips, cut 18 (3⅜") squares. Cut squares in half diagonally to make 36 half-square A triangles (you will have a few extra).

From red print, cut:

• 7 (2¼"-wide) strips for binding.

Block Assembly

1. Choose 3 matching dark print A triangles, 6 matching light print A triangles, and 1 red print B triangle.

2. Join 1 dark print A triangle and 1 light print A triangle as shown in *Triangle-Square Diagrams*. Make 3 triangle-squares.

Triangle-Square Diagrams

3. Lay out triangle-squares, remaining light print A triangles, and red print B triangle as shown in *Block Assembly Diagram* on page 30.

Block Assembly Diagram

4. Join to complete 1 Birds in the Air block *(Block Diagram)*. Make 64 blocks.

Block Diagram

Quilt Assembly

1. Lay out blocks as shown in *Quilt Top Assembly Diagram*.
2. Join into rows; join rows to complete quilt top.

Finishing

1. Divide backing fabric into 2 (1⅞-yard) lengths. Cut 1 piece in half lengthwise to make 2 narrow panels. Join 1 narrow panel to each side of wider panel; press seam allowances toward narrow panels.
2. Layer backing, batting, and quilt top; baste. Quilt as desired. Quilt shown has parallel lines through the red triangles and curved lines in the small triangles *(Quilting Diagram)*.
3. Join 2¼"-wide red print strips into 1 continuous piece for straight-grain French-fold binding. Add binding to quilt.

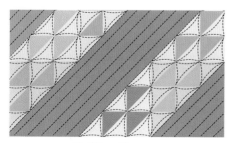

Quilting Diagram

Quilt Top Assembly Diagram

TRIED & TRUE

We used colors that give a contemporary look to this traditional design. Fabrics shown are from the Spice Market collection by Kaye England for Benartex, Inc. and Willowberry Basics by Willowberry Lane for Maywood Studio.

DESIGNER

Jill Reid loves creating scrappy, traditional quilt patterns. She also enjoys making new versions of antique quilts.

Contact her at:

longwood.nj@verizon.net

WEB EXTRA

Go to www.FonsandPorter.com/redsizes to download *Quilt Top Assembly Diagrams* for these size options.

SIZE OPTIONS

	Twin (75" × 90")	Full (90" × 90")	Queen (90" × 105")
Blocks	120 blocks	144 blocks	168 blocks
Setting	10 × 12 blocks	12 × 12 blocks	12 × 14 blocks

MATERIALS

	Twin (75" × 90")	Full (90" × 90")	Queen (90" × 105")
Assorted red prints	15 fat quarters	18 fat quarters	21 fat quarters
Assorted dark prints	10 fat quarters	12 fat quarters	14 fat quarters
Assorted light prints	20 fat quarters	24 fat quarters	28 fat quarters
Red print	¾ yard	¾ yard	⅞ yard
Backing Fabric	5½ yards	8¼ yards	8¼ yards
Batting	Full-size	King-size	King-size

Flag Day

Nothing says summer like the classic combination of red, white, and blue. Sarah Maxwell and Dolores Smith designed this quilt that would be perfect for your summer porch.

PROJECT RATING: INTERMEDIATE
Size: 76" × 94"
Blocks: 63 (9") blocks

MATERIALS

2⅛ yards cream print #1 for blocks
1½ yards cream print #2 for outer border
⅝ yard cream print #3 for blocks
⅜ yard tan print #1 for blocks
½ yard tan print #2 for blocks
½ yard tan print #3 for blocks
½ yard medium blue print #1 for blocks
¾ yard medium blue print #2 for blocks
⅜ yard navy print #1 for blocks
¾ yard navy print #2 for blocks
1 yard navy star print for blocks
¾ yard red stripe for inner border
1 yard red print #1 for blocks and binding
⅜ yard red print #2 for blocks
¾ yard gold print for blocks
Fons & Porter Triangle Trimmers (optional)
7⅛ yards backing fabric
Queen-size quilt batting

Cutting

Measurements include ¼" seam allowances. Border strips are exact length needed. You may want to make them longer to allow for piecing variations.

From cream print #1, cut:
• 2 (5⅜"-wide) strips. From strips, cut 8 (5⅜") squares. Cut squares in half diagonally to make 16 half-square D triangles.

> ### Sew **Smart**™
> Use the blue Fons & Porter Triangle Trimmer to trim D, C, and B triangles. —Marianne

• 4 (4"-wide) strips. From strips, cut 32 (4") squares. Cut squares in half diagonally to make 64 half-square C triangles.
• 16 (2¾"-wide) strips. From strips, cut 80 (2¾" × 5") F rectangles and 80 (2¾") E squares.

From cream print #2, cut:
• 9 (5½"-wide) strips. Piece strips to make 2 (5½" × 84½") side outer borders and 2 (5½" × 76½") top and bottom outer borders.

From cream print #3, cut:
• 1 (5⅜"-wide) strip. From strip, cut 6 (5⅜") squares. Cut squares in half diagonally to make 12 half-square D triangles.
• 3 (4"-wide) strips. From strips, cut 30 (4") squares. Cut squares in half diagonally to make 60 half-square C triangles.

From tan print #1, cut:
• 3 (2¾"-wide) strips for strip sets.

From tan print #2, cut:
• 2 (7¼"-wide) strips. From strips, cut 6 (7¼") G squares.

From tan print #3, cut:
• 2 (7¼"-wide) strips. From strips, cut 6 (7¼") G squares.

From medium blue print #1, cut:
• 3 (3⅝"-wide) strips. From strips, cut 31 (3⅝") A squares.

From medium blue print #2, cut:
• 4 (5⅜"-wide) strips. From strips, cut 24 (5⅜") squares. Cut squares in half diagonally to make 48 half-square D triangles.

From navy print #1, cut:
• 6 (1⅝"-wide) strips. From strips, cut 12 (1⅝" × 9½") I rectangles and 12 (1⅝" × 7¼") H rectangles.

From navy print #2, cut:
- 4 (5⅜"-wide) strips. From strips, cut 24 (5⅜") squares. Cut squares in half diagonally to make 48 half-square D triangles.

From navy star print, cut:
- 12 (2¾"-wide) strips. From strips, cut 160 (2¾") E squares.

From red stripe, cut:
- 8 (2"-wide) strips. Piece strips to make 2 (2" × 81½") side inner borders and 2 (2" × 66½") top and bottom inner borders.

From red print #1, cut:
- 3 (2¾"-wide) strips for strip sets.
- 10 (2¼"-wide) strips for binding.

From red print #2, cut:
- 6 (1⅝"-wide) strips. From strips, cut 12 (1⅝" × 9½") I rectangles and 12 (1⅝" × 7¼") H rectangles.

From gold print, cut:
- 6 (3⅛"-wide) strips. From strips, cut 62 (3⅛") squares. Cut squares in half diagonally to make 24 half-square B triangles.

Block 1 Assembly

1. Join 1 tan print #1 strip and 1 red print #1 strip as shown in *Strip Set Diagram*. Make 3 strip sets. From strip sets, cut 40 (2¾"-wide) segments.

Strip Set Diagram

2. Join 2 segments as shown in *Four Patch Unit Diagrams*. Make 20 Four Patch Units.

Four Patch Unit Diagrams

3. Place 1 navy star print E square atop 1 cream print #1 F rectangle, right sides facing. Stitch diagonally from corner to corner as shown in *Flying Geese Unit Diagrams*. Trim ¼" beyond stitching. Press open to reveal triangle. Repeat for opposite end of rectangle to complete 1 Flying Geese Unit. Make 80 Flying Geese Units.

Flying Geese Unit Diagrams

4. Lay out 1 Four Patch Unit, 4 Flying Geese Units, and 4 cream print #1 E squares as shown in *Block 1 Assembly Diagram*. Join into rows; join rows to complete 1 Block 1 *(Block 1 Diagram)*. Make 20 Block 1.

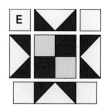

Block 1 Assembly Diagram

Block 1 Diagram

Block 2 Assembly

1. Lay out 1 medium blue print #1 A square, 4 gold print B triangles, and 4 cream print #1 C triangles as shown in *Center Unit Diagrams*. Join pieces

to complete 1 Center Unit. Make 16 Center Units.

Center Unit Diagrams

2. In the same manner, make 15 Center Units using medium blue print #1 A squares, gold print B triangles, and cream print #3 C triangles.

3. Lay out 1 Center Unit with cream print #1 triangles, 2 navy print #2 D triangles, and 2 cream print #1 D triangles as shown in *Block 2 Assembly Diagram*. Join to complete 1 Block 2 *(Block 2 Diagram)*. Make 4 Block 2. Make 4 Block 2 using 2 medium blue print #2 D triangles and 2 cream print #1 D triangles. Make 8 Block 2 using 2 medium blue print #2 D triangles and 2 navy print #2 D triangles.

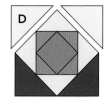

Block 2 Assembly Diagram

Block 2 Diagram

4. In the same manner, make 3 Block 2 using Center Units with cream print #3 triangles, 2 navy print #2

D triangles, and 2 cream print #3 D triangles. Make 3 Block 2 using 2 medium blue print #2 D triangles and 2 cream print #3 D triangles. Make 9 Block 2 using 2 medium blue print #2 D triangles and 2 navy print #2 D triangles.

Block 3 Assembly

1. Lay out 1 tan print #3 G square, 2 red print #2 H rectangles, and 2 red print #2 I rectangles as shown in *Block 3 Assembly Diagram*. Join pieces to complete 1 Block 3 (*Block 3 Diagram*). Make 6 Block 3.

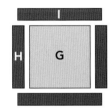

Block 3 Assembly Diagram

Block 3 Diagram

2. In the same manner, make 6 Block 3 using 1 tan print #2 G square, 2 navy print #1 H rectangles, and 2 navy print #1 I rectangles.

Quilt Assembly

1. Lay out blocks as shown in *Quilt Top Assembly Diagram*. Join into rows, join rows to complete quilt center.

2. Add red stripe side inner borders to quilt center. Add red stripe top and bottom inner borders to quilt.

3. Repeat for cream print #2 outer borders.

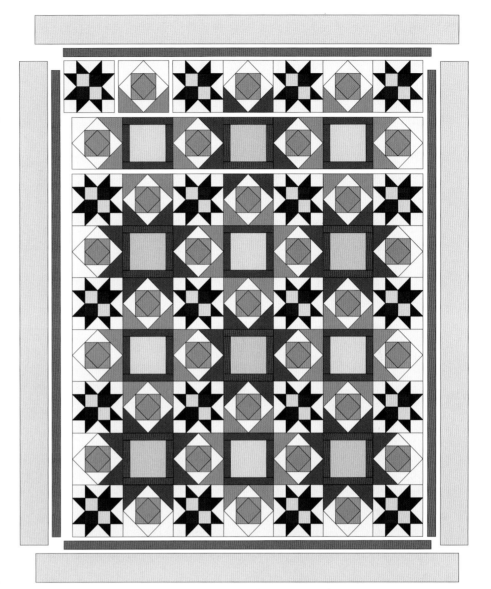

Quilt Top Assembly Diagram

Finishing

1. Divide backing into 3 (2⅜-yard) lengths. Join panels lengthwise. Seams will run horizontally.

2. Layer backing, batting, and quilt top; baste. Quilt as desired. Quilt shown was quilted with a variety of motifs in the blocks, and swirl and scroll designs in the borders (*Quilting Diagram*).

3. Join 2¼"-wide red print strips into 1 continuous piece for straight-grain French-fold binding. Add binding to quilt.

Quilting Diagram

TRIED & TRUE

Our version features large-scale prints from the Fleurs Tulips collection by Marjorie Post and Dimples by Gail Kessler. Both fabric collections are from Andover Fabrics.

SIZE OPTION

	Throw (58" × 76")
Setting	5 × 7
Block 1	12
Block 2	17
Block 3	6

DESIGNER

Sarah Maxwell and Dolores Smith, owners of Homestead Hearth™ pattern company, have a passion for creating original patterns using many prints from their stash or from a single fabric line.

Contact them at:

info@homesteadhearth.com

www.homesteadhearth.com ✳

MATERIALS

Cream Print #1	1½ yards
Cream Print #2	1⅜ yards
Cream Print #3	⅝ yard
Tan Print #1	¼ yard
Tan Print #2	¼ yard
Tan Print #3	¼ yard
Medium Blue Print #1	¼ yard
Medium Blue Print #2	⅝ yard
Navy Print #1	¼ yard
Navy Print #2	⅝ yard
Navy Star Print #1	¾ yard
Red Stripe	½ yard
Red Print #1	¾ yard
Red Print #2	¼ yard
Gold Print	⅜ yard
Backing Fabric	3¾ yards
Batting	Twin-size

QUILT DESIGNED BY **Judy Martin**.
MADE BY **Chris Hulin**. MACHINE QUILTED BY **Margy Sieck**.

Echoing Stars

Judy Martin combined traditional Flying Geese units, Evening Star blocks, and Rising Star blocks to make a quilt that sparkles!

PROJECT RATING: CHALLENGING
Size: 102" × 102"
Blocks: 25 (18") blocks

MATERIALS

NOTE: Number blue, red, and orange fabrics from light to dark.

⅜ yard blue print #1
½ yard blue print #2
1⅜ yards blue print #3
2 yards blue print #4
3⅛ yards blue print #5
1¾ yards blue print #6
⅝ yard red print #1
⅞ yard red print #2
⅜ yard red print #3
½ yard red print #4

⅝ yard yellow print
⅜ yard orange print #1
¾ yard orange print #2
¾ yard orange print #3
¾ yard orange print #4
1⅜ yards orange print #5
⅞ yard medium blue print for binding
Template material
9 yards backing fabric
King-size quilt batting

Cutting

Measurements include ¼" seam allowances. Patterns for templates are on page 45. Border strips are exact length needed. You may want to make them longer to allow for piecing variations.

From blue print #1, cut:

• 1 (4¼"-wide) strip. From strip, cut 8 (4¼") squares. Cut squares in half diagonally in both directions to make 32 quarter-square E triangles.
• 2 (2"-wide) strips. From strips, cut 32 (2") B squares.

From blue print #2, cut:
- 7 (2"-wide) strips. From strips, cut 32 H and 32 H reversed.

From blue print #3, cut:
- 22 (2"-wide) strips. From strips, cut 64 (2") B squares, 32 F, 32 F reversed, 32 I, and 32 I reversed.

From blue print #4, cut:
- 33 (2"-wide) strips. From strips, cut 72 (2") B squares, 36 F, 36 F reversed, 64 J, and 64 J reversed.

From blue print #5, cut:
- 54 (2"-wide) strips. From strips, cut 144 (2") B squares, 36 G, 36 G reversed, 64 K, and 64 K reversed. Piece remaining strips to make 2 (2" × 99½") side borders and 2 (2" × 102½") top and bottom borders.

From blue print #6, cut:
- 30 (2"-wide) strips. From strips, cut 60 (2" × 18½") sashing strips.

From red print #1, cut:
- 2 (4¼"-wide) strips. From strips, cut 17 (4¼") squares. Cut squares in half diagonally in both directions to make 68 quarter-square E triangles.
- 4 (2"-wide) strips. From strips, cut 68 (2") B squares.

From red print #2, cut:
- 7 (3⅞"-wide) strips. From strips, cut 68 (3⅞") squares. Cut squares in half diagonally to make 136 half-square D triangles.

From red print #3, cut:
- 3 (3½"-wide) strips. From strips, cut 25 (3½") A squares.

From red print #4, cut:
- 7 (2⅜"-wide) strips. From strips, cut 100 (2⅜") squares. Cut squares in half diagonally to make 200 half-square C triangles.

From yellow print, cut:
- 2 (4¼"-wide) strips. From strips, cut 16 (4¼") squares. Cut squares in half diagonally in both directions to make 64 quarter-square E triangles.
- 4 (2"-wide) strips. From strips, cut 64 (2") B squares.

From orange print #1, cut:
- 1 (4¼"-wide) strip. From strip, cut 9 (4¼") squares. Cut squares in half diagonally in both directions to make 36 quarter-square E triangles.
- 2 (2"-wide) strips. From strips, cut 36 (2") B squares.

From orange print #2, cut:
- 3 (4¼"-wide) strips. From strips, cut 25 (4¼") squares. Cut squares in half diagonally in both directions to make 100 quarter-square E triangles.
- 5 (2"-wide) strips. From strips, cut 100 (2") B squares.

From orange print #3, cut:
- 3 (4¼"-wide) strips. From strips, cut 25 (4¼") squares. Cut squares in half diagonally in both directions to make 100 quarter-square E triangles.
- 5 (2"-wide) strips. From strips, cut 100 (2") B squares.

From orange print #4, cut:
- 3 (4¼"-wide) strips. From strips, cut 25 (4¼") squares. Cut squares in half diagonally in both directions to make 100 quarter-square E triangles.
- 5 (2"-wide) strips. From strips, cut 100 (2") B squares.

From orange print #5, cut:
- 4 (3⅞"-wide) strips. From strips, cut 36 (3⅞") squares. Cut squares in half diagonally to make 72 half-square D triangles.
- 14 (2"-wide) strips. From strips, cut 108 (2") B squares, 36 F, and 36 F reversed. (Set aside 36 B squares for sashing.)

From medium blue print, cut:
- 12 (2¼"-wide) strips for binding.

Center Unit Assembly

1. Lay out 1 red #3 A square, 8 red #4 C triangles, 4 blue #1 B squares, and 4 blue #1 E triangles as shown in *Center Unit 1 Assembly Diagram*. Join into rows; join rows to complete 1 Center Unit 1 (*Center Unit 1 Diagram*). Make 8 Center Unit 1.

Center Unit 1 Assembly Diagram

Center Unit 1 Diagram

2. In the same manner, join 1 red #3 A square, 8 red #4 C triangles, 4 red #1 B squares, and 4 red #1 E triangles to make 1 Center Unit 2 (*Center Unit 2 Diagram*). Make 17 Center Unit 2.

Center Unit 2 Diagram

Side Unit Assembly

1. Lay out 2 red #2 D triangles, 1 yellow E triangle, 1 orange #2 E triangle, 1 blue #3 F, and 1 blue #3 F reversed as shown in *Block 2 Side Unit Assembly Diagram*. Join into sections; join sections as shown in *Block 2 Side Unit Diagram*. Make 32 Block 2 Side Units.

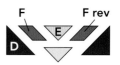

Block 2 Side Unit Assembly Diagram

Block 2 Side Unit Diagram

2. In the same manner, join 2 red #2 D triangles, 1 orange #1 E triangle, 1 orange #2 E triangle, 1 orange #5 F, and 1 orange #5 F reversed as shown in *Block 3 Short Side Unit Diagram*. Make 36 Block 3 Short Side Units.

Block 3 Short Side Unit Diagram

3. Join 2 orange #5 D triangles, 1 orange #3 E triangle, 1 orange #4 E triangle, 1 blue #4 F, 1 blue #4 F reversed, 1 blue #5 G, 1 blue #5 G reversed, 2 blue #4 B squares, and 2 blue #5 B squares as shown in *Block 3 Long Side Unit Diagram*. Make 36 Block 3 Long Side Units.

Block 3 Long Side Unit Diagram

Four Patch Assembly

1. Join 1 orange #2 B square, 1 yellow B square, and 2 blue #3 B squares as shown in *Block 2 Four Patch Unit Diagram*. Make 32 Block 2 Four Patch Units.

Block 2 Four Patch Unit Diagram

2. In the same manner, join 1 orange #2 B square, 1 orange #1 B square, and 2 orange #5 B squares as shown in *Block 3 Four Patch Unit Diagrams*. Make 36 Block 3 Four Patch Units in these colors.

Block 3 Four Patch Unit Diagrams

3. Join 1 orange #4 B square, 1 orange #3 B square, and 2 blue #5 B squares as shown in *Block 3 Four Patch Unit Diagrams*. Make 36 Block 3 Four Patch Units in these colors.

Block 1 Assembly

1. Referring to *Block 1 Assembly Diagram*, lay out 1 Center Unit 1, 4 blue #2 H and H reversed pieces, 4 blue #3 I and I reversed pieces, 4 blue #4 J and J reversed pieces, 4 blue #5 K and K reversed pieces, and 1 set of 4 E triangles and 4 B squares each in yellow, orange #2, orange #3, and orange #4.

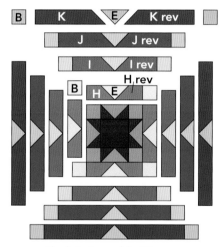

Block 1 Assembly Diagram

2. Join into sections; join sections to complete 1 Block 1 *(Block 1 Diagram)*. Make 8 Block 1.

Block 1 Diagram

Block 2 Assembly

1. Referring to *Block 2 Assembly Diagram*, lay out 1 Center Unit 2, 4 Block 2 Side Units, 4 Block 2 Four Patch Units, 4 blue #4 J and J reversed pieces, 4 blue #5 K and K reversed pieces, and 1 set of 4 E triangles and 4 B squares each in orange #3 and orange #4.

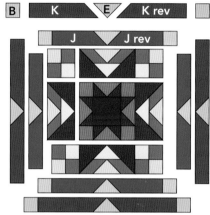

Block 2 Assembly Diagram

2. Join into sections; join sections to complete 1 Block 2 *(Block 2 Diagram)*. Make 8 Block 2.

Block 2 Diagram

Block 3 Assembly

1. Referring to *Block 3 Assembly Diagram* on page 42, lay out 1 Center Unit 2, 4 Block 3 Short Side Units, 4 Block 3 Long Side Units, and 8 Block 3 Four Patch Units.

Block 3 Assembly Diagram

2. Join into sections; join sections to complete 1 Block 3 *(Block 3 Diagram)*. Make 9 Block 3.

Block 3 Diagram

Quilt Assembly

1. Lay out blocks, sashing strips, and B sashing squares as shown in *Quilt Top Assembly Diagram* on page 43. Join into rows; join rows to complete quilt center.
2. Add side borders to quilt center. Add top and bottom borders to quilt.

Finishing

1. Divide backing fabric into 3 (3-yard) lengths. Join pieces lengthwise.
2. Layer backing, batting, and quilt top; baste. Quilt as desired. Quilt shown was machine quilted with straight lines in a diagonal grid through the B squares and concentric circles in each block *(Quilting Diagram)*.
3. Join 2¼"-wide medium blue print strips into 1 continuous piece for straight-grain French-fold binding. Add binding to quilt.

Quilting Diagram

TRIED & TRUE

The reproduction fabrics used here give this block an antique look.

Quilt Top Assembly Diagram

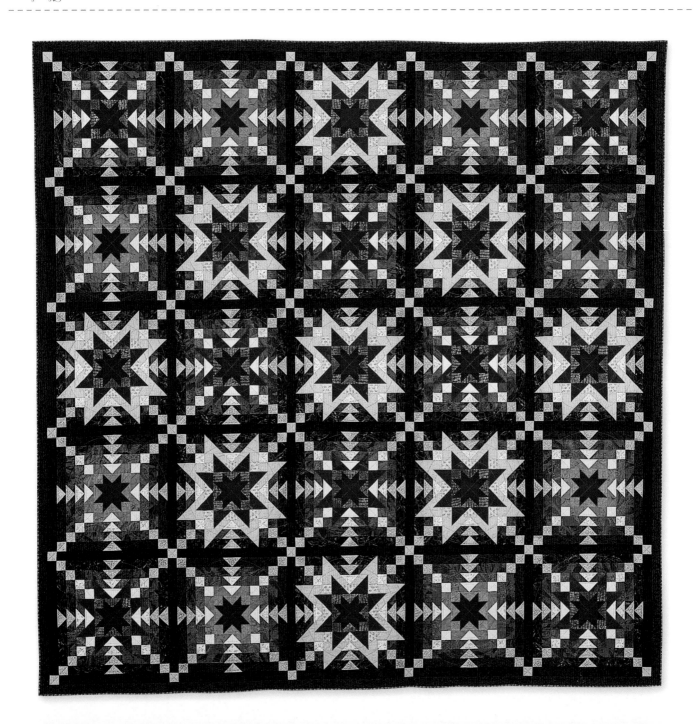

DESIGNER

Judy Martin loves the design process of quiltmaking and has earned high esteem for her beautiful quilts. Author of many popular books, Judy's most recent release is *Stellar Quilts*, a book of thirteen great patterns.

Contact her at:

www.JudyMartin.com ✳

Heart of America

Sisters Lynn Witzenburg and Cindi Hayes got together one weekend to design and make this spirited Americana wall quilt for Cindi's newly decorated family room. Both love stars, so they had a blast including lots of star prints.

Size: 55" × 43"

MATERIALS

2 fat eighths★ dark blue prints for flag star field, heart appliqués, and stars

⅛ yard each of 2 red prints for stripes, heart appliqués, and stars

3 fat eighths★ assorted red prints for stripes, heart appliqués, and stars

1⅛ yards cream print for star border rectangles, flag stripes, and stars

⅜ yard gold print for flag border and stars

⅜ yard beige print for heart appliqué backgrounds

½ yard dark red print for sashing and stars

1⅛ yards dark blue print for border, binding, and stars

1 fat eighth★ blue stripe for heart appliqués

Paper-backed fusible web

2¾ yards backing fabric

Twin-size batting

★fat eighth = 9" × 20"

Cutting

Measurements include ¼" seam allowances. Border strips are exact length needed. You may want to cut them longer to allow for piecing variations. Appliqué patterns are on pages 50–51.

Follow manufacturer's instructions for using fusible web.

From 1 dark blue print fat eighth, cut:

• 1 (12¼" × 8½") rectangle.

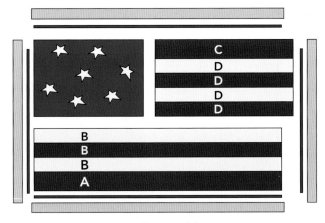
Flag Block Assembly Diagram

From red print #1, cut:
- 1 (2½" × 27") flag stripe A.

From red print #2, cut:
- 1 (2" × 27") flag stripe B.

From assorted red print fat eighths, cut a total of:
- 1 (2½" × 15¼") flag stripe C and 2 (2" × 15¼") flag stripe D.
- 2 Star #2.
- 1 Star #3.
- 1 Star #4.
- 3 Star #5.
- 4 Heart piece #2.
- 4 Heart piece #4.
- 4 Heart piece #5.

From cream print, cut:
- 3 (2"-wide) strips. From strips, cut 2 (2" × 27") flag stripe B and 2 (2" × 15¼") flag stripe D.
- 3 (9½"-wide) strips. From strips, cut 2 (9½" × 29½") top and bottom star border rectangles and 2 (9½" ×17½") side star border rectangles.
- 11 Star #5.

From gold print, cut:
- 3 (1½"-wide) strips. From strips, cut 2 (1½" × 27½") top and bottom flag borders and 2 (1½" × 17½") side flag borders.
- 10 Star #3.
- 5 Star #4.

From beige print, cut:
- 4 (9½") squares for heart appliqué backgrounds.

From dark red print, cut:
- 9 (1"-wide) strips. From strips, cut 2 (1" × 17½") vertical sashing strips, 4 (1" × 9½") vertical sashing strips, and 2 (1" × 37½") vertical sashing strips. Piece remaining strips to make 4 (1" × 48½") horizontal sashing strips.

From dark blue print, cut:
- 3 (¾"-wide) strips. From strips, cut 2 (¾" × 27") top and bottom flag borders and 2 (¾" × 15½") side flag borders.
- 5 (3½"-wide) strips. Piece strips to make 2 (3½" × 49½") top and bottom outer borders and 2 (3½" × 43½") side outer borders.
- 6 (2¼"-wide) strips for binding.

From dark blue prints, cut a total of:
- 4 Star #1.
- 6 Star #2.
- 4 Star #3.
- 3 Star #4.
- 4 Star #5.
- 4 Heart piece #1.

From blue stripe fat eighth, cut:
- 4 Heart piece #3.
- 4 Heart piece #6.

Flag Block Assembly

1. Position 7 cream Star #5 atop dark blue print rectangle as shown in *Flag Block Assembly Diagram*. Fuse in place. Machine appliqué using matching thread.
2. Lay out rectangle and flag stripes as shown in *Flag Block Assembly Diagram*. Join into sections; join sections to complete flag.
3. Add dark blue print top and bottom flag borders to flag. Add dark blue side flag borders.
4. Repeat for gold print flag borders.

Heart Block Assembly

1. Position 6 heart pieces, 1 cream Star #5, 1 gold Star #3, and 1 gold Star #4 on 1 beige background square as shown in *Heart Block Diagram*. Fuse in place.

Heart Block Diagram

2. Machine appliqué using matching thread to complete 1 Heart block. Make 4 Heart blocks.

Star Border Assembly

1. Referring to *Quilt Top Assembly Diagram*, divide the remaining 35 stars among the 2 top and bottom star border rectangles and 2 side star border rectangles, placing 1 blue Star #1 on each rectangle.

Quilt Top Assembly Diagram

2. Fuse pieces in place. Machine appliqué using matching thread.

Quilt Assembly

1. Lay out flag, Heart blocks, star border rectangles, and red sashing strips. Join into rows; join rows. Add 1" × 37½" vertical sashing strips to sides to complete quilt center.

2. Add dark blue print top and bottom outer borders to quilt. Add dark blue print side outer borders to quilt.

Finishing

1. Divide backing fabric into 2 (1⅜-yard) lengths. Cut 1 piece in half lengthwise to make 2 narrow panels. Sew 1 narrow panel to wider panel; press seam allowance toward narrow panel. Remaining panel is extra and can be used to make a hanging sleeve.

2. Layer backing, batting, and quilt top; baste. Quilt as desired. Quilt shown was quilted in the ditch between sections, with a star pattern in the star border rectangles, a grid in the Heart blocks, and wiggly lines in the flag stripes.

3. Join 2¼"-wide dark blue print strips into 1 continuous piece for straight-grain French-fold binding. Add binding to quilt.

DESIGNER

Lynn Witzenburg has been quilting since 1979. She has a custom machine quilting business and also loves to teach machine quilting and dimensional hand appliqué and give quilt lectures. Look for her book, *Machine Quilting: The Basics and Beyond*, published by Landauer Publishing. Lynn lives in Des Moines, Iowa. ✳

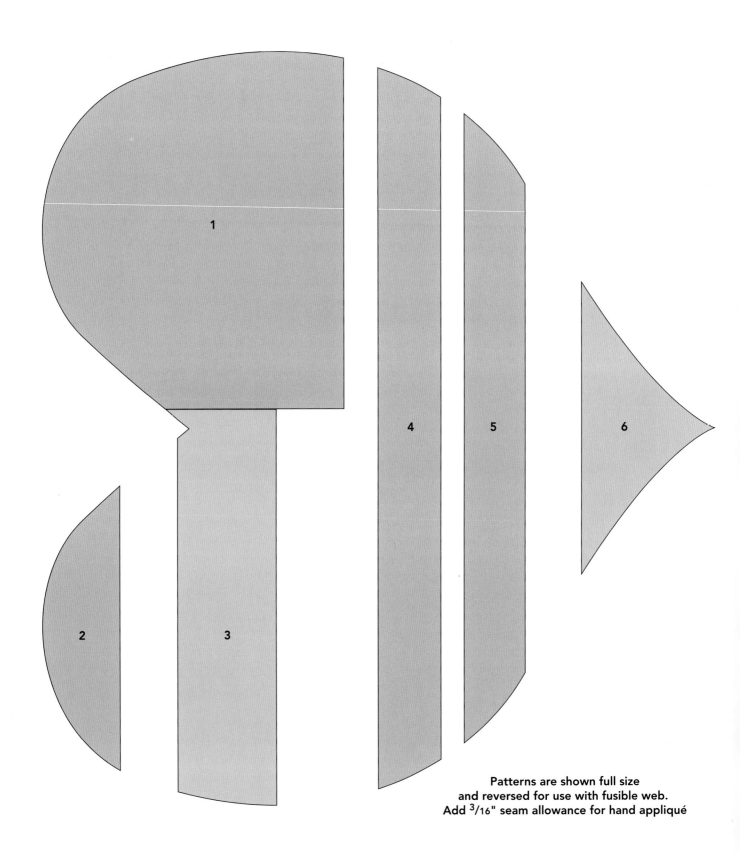

1

2

3

4

5

6

Patterns are shown full size
and reversed for use with fusible web.
Add $3/16$" seam allowance for hand appliqué

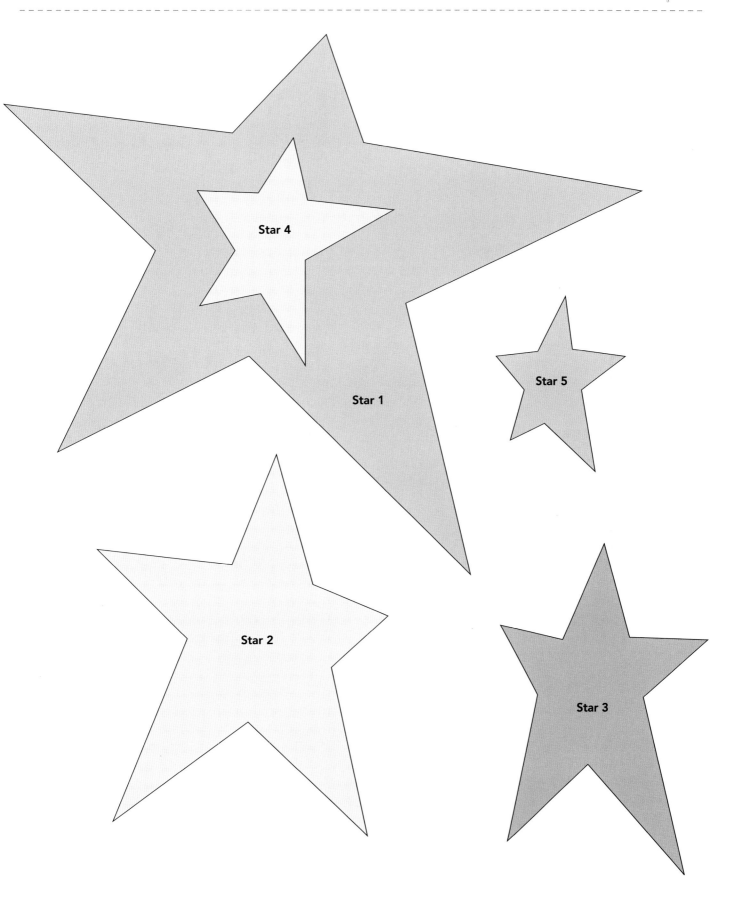

Star 4

Star 1

Star 5

Star 2

Star 3

QUILT DESIGNED AND MACHINE QUILTED BY **Cyndi Walker**.

PIECED BY **Debbie Gray**.

Glory Days

Designer Cyndi Walker created this quilt that's bursting with color.
It's perfect to take on a picnic or to the fireworks.

PROJECT RATING: EASY

Size: 52" × 68"

Blocks: 18 (8") Star blocks
17 (8") Nine Patch blocks

MATERIALS

1⅛ yards navy print for Star blocks

1 yard light blue print for Star
blocks and binding

½ yard light blue dots for inner
border

1⅛ yards white dots for Star blocks

½ yard red print for Nine Patch
blocks

1⅜ yards white print for Nine
Patch blocks and outer border

1 yard red dots for Nine Patch
blocks and outer border

Fons & Porter Quarter Inch Seam
Marker (optional)

3¼ yards backing fabric

Twin-size quilt batting

Cutting

Measurements include ¼" seam
allowances. Border strips are exact
length needed. You may want to make
them longer to allow for piecing
variations.

From navy print fabric, cut:

• 5 (4½"-wide) strips. From strips, cut
72 (4½" × 2½") C rectangles.

• 5 (2½"-wide) strips. From strips, cut
72 (2½") B squares.

From light blue print, cut:

• 3 (4½"-wide) strips. From strips, cut
18 (4½") A squares.

• 7 (2¼"-wide) strips for binding.

From light blue dots, cut:

• 6 (2½"-wide) strips. Piece strips to
make 2 (2½" × 56½") side inner
borders and 2 (2½" × 44½") top and
bottom inner borders.

From white dots, cut:

• 14 (2½"-wide) strips. From strips, cut
216 (2½") B squares.

From red print, cut:

• 3 (4½"-wide) strips. From strips, cut
17 (4½") A squares.

From white print, cut:

• 4 (4⅞"-wide) strips. From strips, cut
28 (4⅞") D squares.

• 5 (4½"-wide) strips. From strips, cut
68 (4½" × 2½") C rectangles.

Sew **Smart**™

Stack 1 (4⅞"-wide) white print
strip and 1 (4⅞"-wide) red dot
strip, right sides facing. Cut (4⅞")
squares from stacked strips. Keep
pairs together to make triangle-
squares. See *Sew Easy: Quick Half-
Square Triangle Units* on page 57.

From red dots, cut:

• 4 (4⅞"-wide) strips. From strips, cut
28 (4⅞") D squares.

• 5 (2½"-wide) strips. From strips, cut
68 (2½") B squares.

Block Assembly

1. Referring to *Block Center Diagrams*,
place 1 white dot B square atop 1
light blue print A square, right sides
facing. Stitch diagonally from corner
to corner as shown. Trim ¼" beyond
stitching. Press open to reveal triangle.
Repeat for 3 remaining corners to
complete 1 Block Center. Make 18
Block Centers.

Block Center Diagrams

2. Referring to *Flying Geese Unit Diagrams*, place 1 white dot B square atop 1 navy print C rectangle, right sides facing. Stitch diagonally from corner to corner as shown. Trim ¼" beyond stitching. Press open to reveal triangle. Repeat for opposite corner to complete 1 Flying Geese Unit. Make 72 Flying Geese Units.

Flying Geese Unit Diagrams

3. Lay out 1 Block Center, 4 Flying Geese Units, and 4 navy print B squares as shown in *Star Block Assembly Diagram*. Join into rows; join rows to complete 1 Star block *(Star Block Diagram)*. Make 18 Star blocks.

Star Block Assembly Diagram　　Star Block Diagram

4. Lay out 1 red print A square, 4 red dot B squares, and 4 white print C rectangles as shown in *Nine Patch Block Assembly Diagram*. Join into rows; join rows to complete 1 Nine Patch block *(Nine Patch Block Diagram)*. Make 17 Nine Patch blocks.

Nine Patch Block Assembly Diagram　　Nine Patch Block Diagram

5. Using red dot D squares and white print D squares, make 56 triangle-squares as shown in *Triangle-Square Diagram*. Refer to *Sew Easy: Quick Half-Square Triangle Units* on page 57 for an accurate way to mark sewing lines for these units.

Triangle-Square Diagram

Quilt Top Assembly Diagram

Quilt Assembly

1. Lay out blocks as shown in *Quilt Top Assembly Diagram*. Join into rows; join rows to complete quilt center.

2. Add blue dot side inner borders to quilt center. Add top and bottom inner borders to quilt.

3. Referring to *Quilt Top Assembly Diagram*, lay out 15 triangle-squares as shown. Join to make 1 pieced side border. Make 2 pieced side borders.

4. In the same manner, join 13 triangle-squares to make pieced top border. Repeat for pieced bottom border.

5. Add pieced side borders to quilt center. Add pieced top and bottom borders to quilt.

Finishing

1. Divide backing into 2 (1⅝-yard) lengths. Join panels lengthwise. Seam will run horizontally.

2. Layer backing, batting, and quilt top; baste. Quilt as desired. Quilt shown was quilted with an allover swirl design *(Quilting Diagram)*.

3. Join 2¼"-wide light blue print strips into 1 continuous piece for straight-grain French-fold binding. Add binding to quilt.

Quilting Diagram

TRIED & TRUE

The garden is in full bloom in our summery version of these blocks. Fabrics shown are from the Amma's Garden collection by Gudrun Erla for Red Rooster Fabrics.

SIZE OPTIONS

	Crib (36" × 36")	Twin (68" × 84")	Full/Queen (84" × 100")
Star Blocks	5	32	50
Nine Patch Blocks	4	31	49
Setting	3 × 3	7 × 9	9 × 11

MATERIALS

	Crib (36" × 36")	Twin (68" × 84")	Full/Queen (84" × 100")
Navy Print	½ yard	1¾ yards	2⅝ yards
Light Blue Print	⅝ yard	1⅜ yards	1⅞ yards
Light Blue Dots	⅜ yard	⅝ yard	¾ yard
White Dots	⅜ yard	1¾ yards	2⅞ yards
Red Print	¼ yard	⅝ yard	1 yard
White Print	½ yard	1¾ yards	2⅝ yards
Red Dots	⅜ yard	1½ yards	2¼ yards
Backing Fabric	1¼ yards	5 yards	7½ yards
Batting	Crib-size	Twin-size	Queen-size

 WEB EXTRA
Go to www.FonsandPorter.com/glorydayssizes to download *Quilt Top Assembly Diagrams* for these size options.

DESIGNER

Cyndi Walker is a quilt designer, teacher, and author who lives near Seattle, Washington. Her pattern company, Stitch Studios, features original, fun, and easy quilt patterns that incorporate her love for scrap quilts and appliqué. Look for her book, *Spotlight on Scraps*, published by Martingale & Company.

Contact her at: Stitch Studios • www.stitchstudios.com ✳

Quick Half-Square Triangle Units

The Fons & Porter Quarter Inch Seam Marker offers a neat way to mark accurate sewing lines for Half-Square Triangle Units.

A

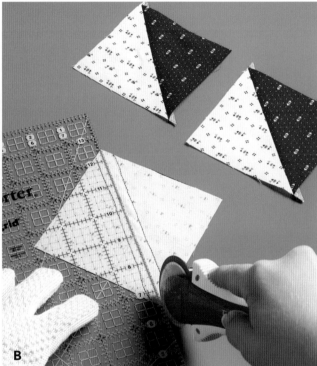

B

1. From each of 2 fabrics, cut 1 square ⅞" larger than the desired finished size of the Half-Square Triangle Unit. For example, to make a Half-Square Triangle Unit that will finish 4" as in the *Glory Days* quilt, cut 4⅞" squares.

2. On wrong side of lighter square, place the Quarter Inch Seam Marker diagonally across the square, with the yellow center line positioned exactly on opposite corners. Mark stitching lines along both sides of the Quarter Inch Seam Marker (*Photo A*).

NOTE: If not using the Quarter Inch Seam Marker, draw a diagonal line from corner to corner on lighter square. Then draw lines ¼" away on each side of the first line.

3. Place light square atop darker square, right sides facing; stitch along both marked sewing lines.

4. Cut between rows of stitching to make 2 Half-Square Triangle Units (*Photo B*).

Blackbird Crossing

This traditional quilt features crows, stars, pinwheels, and shirting prints. Easy fusible appliqué and quick cutting using the Fons & Porter Flying Geese Ruler help you finish it quickly.

PROJECT RATING: INTERMEDIATE

Size: 60" × 72"

Blocks: 90 (6") Pinwheel blocks

MATERIALS

⅝ yard cream print for center

16 fat quarters★★ assorted light prints

11 fat quarters★★ assorted red prints

12 fat quarters★★ assorted blue prints

2 fat eighths★ black prints

⅝ yard red print for binding

Fons & Porter Flying Geese Ruler (optional)

Paper-backed fusible web

4 yards backing fabric

Twin-size quilt batting

★fat eighth = 9" × 20"

★★fat quarter = 18" × 20"

Cutting

Measurements include ¼" seam allowances. Border strips are exact length needed. You may want to make them longer to allow for piecing variations. Patterns for appliqué shapes are on page 63. Follow manufacturer's instructions for using fusible web. Instructions are written for using the Fons & Porter Flying Geese Ruler. If not using the Fons & Porter Flying Geese Ruler, follow cutting **NOTES**.

From cream print, cut:

• 1 (18½") A square.

From each of 13 light print fat quarters, cut:

• 4 (3½"-wide) strips. From strips, cut 32 half-square D triangles.

   NOTE: If NOT using the Fons & Porter Flying Geese Ruler, cut: 4 (3⅞"-wide) strips. From strips, cut 16 (3⅞") squares. Cut squares in half diagonally to make 32 half-square D triangles.

From remaining light print fat quarters, cut a total of:

• 10 (6½") B squares.

From each of 7 red print fat quarters, cut:

• 4 (3½"-wide) strips. From strips, cut 16 half-square D triangles and 6 quarter-square E triangles.

   NOTE: If NOT using the Fons & Porter Flying Geese Ruler, cut: 2 (3⅞"-wide) strips. From strips, cut 8 (3⅞") squares. Cut squares in half diagonally to make 16 half-square D triangles; and cut 1 (7¼"-wide) strip, from strip, cut 2 (7¼") squares. Cut squares in half diagonally in both directions to make 8 quarter-square E triangles.

From each remaining red print fat quarter, cut:

• 1 (3½"-wide) strip. From strip, cut 1 (3½") C square.

- 1 (3½"-wide) strip. From strip, cut 8 half-square D triangles.

  NOTE: If NOT using the Fons & Porter Flying Geese Ruler, cut: 1 (3⅞"-wide) strip. From strip, cut 4 (3⅞") squares. Cut squares in half diagonally to make 8 half-square D triangles.

- 1 Star.
- 1 Flower.

From 1 blue print fat quarter, cut:

- 1 Center Circle.

From 1 blue print fat quarter, cut:

- 1 (3½"-wide) strip. From strip, cut 4 (3½") C squares.
- 4 Stems.
- 8 Leaves.

From each of 4 blue print fat quarters, cut:

- 4 (3½"-wide) strips. From strips, cut 32 half-square D triangles.

  NOTE: If NOT using the Fons & Porter Flying Geese Ruler, cut: 4 (3⅞"-wide) strips. From strips, cut 16 (3⅞") squares. Cut squares in half diagonally to make 32 half-square D triangles.

From each of 6 blue print fat quarters, cut:

- 1 (3½"-wide) strip. From strip, cut 8 half-square D triangles.

  NOTE: If NOT using the Fons & Porter Flying Geese Ruler, cut: 1 (3⅞"-wide) strip. From strip, cut 4 (3⅞") squares. Cut squares in half diagonally to make 8 half-square D triangles.

- 1 Star.

From each black fat eighth, cut:

- 2 Birds.
- 2 Flower Centers.

From red print, cut:

- 8 (2¼"-wide) strips for binding.

Center Assembly

1. Referring to *Diagonal Seams Diagrams*, place 1 blue print C square atop cream print A square, right sides facing. Stitch diagonally from corner to corner as shown. Trim ¼" beyond stitching. Press open to reveal triangle. Repeat for remaining corners to make center square background.

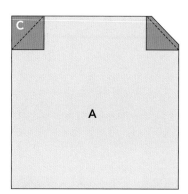

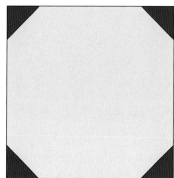

Diagonal Seams Diagrams

2. Position appliqué pieces on center square background as shown in *Quilt Top Assembly Diagram* on page 61. Appliqué pieces on background to complete center square.

Star Block Assembly

1. Appliqué 1 red star on 1 light print B square to complete 1 Star block. Make 4 red Star blocks *(Star Block Diagrams)*.

2. In the same manner, make 6 blue Star blocks.

Star Block Diagrams

Pinwheel Block Assembly

1. Choose 4 matching red print D triangles and 4 matching light print D triangles. Join 1 red triangle and 1 light triangle as shown in *Triangle-Square Diagrams*. Make 4 triangle-squares.

Triangle-Square Diagrams

> **Sew Smart™**
> Press seams open on triangle-squares to eliminate the bump where 8 triangles meet. —Liz

2. Lay out 4 triangle-squares as shown in *Pinwheel Block Assembly Diagram*. Join to make 1 Pinwheel block *(Pinwheel Block Diagram)*. Make 36 red Pinwheel blocks.

Pinwheel Block Assembly Diagram   Pinwheel Block Diagram

3. In the same manner, make 44 blue Pinwheel blocks.

Border Assembly

1. Choose 2 matching light print D triangles and 1 red print E triangle. Join pieces as shown in *Flying Geese Unit Diagrams*. Make 40 Flying Geese Units.

Flying Geese Unit Diagrams

2. Lay out 11 Flying Geese Units as shown in *Quilt Top Assembly Diagram*. Join to make 1 side border. Make 2 side borders.

3. In the same manner, join 9 Flying Geese Units to make top border. Repeat for bottom border.

Quilt Assembly

1. Lay out Center Square and blocks as shown in *Quilt Top Assembly Diagram*. Join into rows; join rows to complete quilt center.

2. Add side borders to quilt center.

3. Add 1 red print C square to each end of top and bottom borders. Add borders to quilt.

Finishing

1. Divide backing into 2 (2-yard) lengths. Join panels lengthwise. Seam will run horizontally.

2. Layer backing, batting, and quilt top; baste. Quilt as desired. Quilt shown was outline quilted around appliqué pieces and has curved lines in Pinwheel blocks *(Quilting Diagram)*.

3. Join 2¼"-wide red print strips into 1 continuous piece for straight-grain French-fold binding. Add binding to quilt.

Quilt Top Assembly Diagram

Quilting Diagram

SIZE OPTION

	Wallhanging (42" × 42")
Pinwheel Blocks	36

MATERIALS

Light Print	⅝ yard
Light Prints	8 fat quarters
Red Prints	8 fat quarters
Blue Prints	2 fat quarters
Binding	½ yard
Backing Fabric	2¾ yards
Batting	Crib-size

 WEB EXTRA

Go to www.FonsandPorter.com/blackbirdsize to download *Quilt Top Assembly Diagram* for this size option.

DESIGNER

Susan McDermott, a folk art painter from Warren, New Jersey, began designing her own quilts shortly after learning to quilt about twenty years ago.

Contact her at:

suemcd1@optonline.net ✳

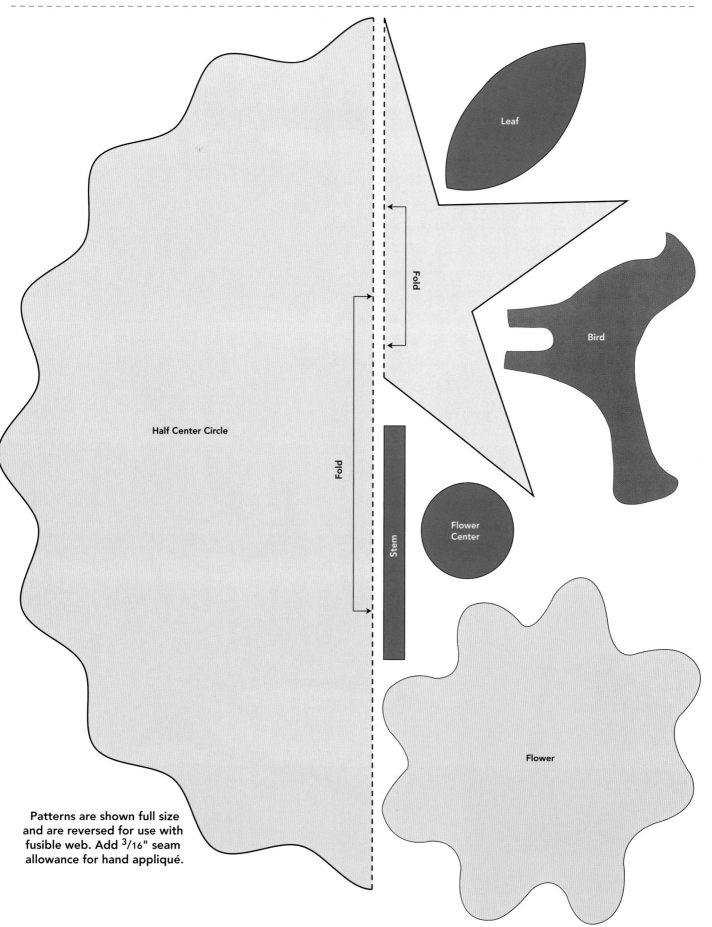

Leaf

Fold

Bird

Half Center Circle

Fold

Stem

Flower
Center

Flower

Patterns are shown full size
and are reversed for use with
fusible web. Add $^3/16$" seam
allowance for hand appliqué.

QUILT BY **Lori Hein**.
MACHINE QUILTED BY **Wanda Jeffries**.

Bandana Beauty

Use a traditional bandana print in classic trefoil and paisley shapes to make this easy appliqué quilt.

Size: 56" × 72"

MATERIALS

1¼ yards red print for blocks and appliqué

1¼ yards blue print for blocks and appliqué

2½ yards cream print for background (must be at least 40½" wide)

¾ yard dark red print for blocks and appliqué

1 yard dark blue print for blocks, appliqué, and binding

Paper-backed fusible web

Dark blue pearl cotton

3½ yards backing fabric

Twin-size quilt batting

Cutting

Measurements include ¼" seam allowances. Patterns for appliqué pieces are on pages 68–69. Follow manufacturer's instructions for using fusible web.

From red print, cut:

• 3 (8½"-wide) strips. From strips, cut 9 (8½") F squares.

• 4 A.

• 8 D.

From blue print, cut:

• 3 (8½"-wide) strips. From strips, cut 11 (8½") F squares.

• 8 B.

• 8 B reversed.

From cream print, cut:

• 1 (40½"-wide) strip. From strip, cut 1 (40½") square.

• 5 (4½"-wide) strips. From strips, cut 36 (4½") G squares.

• 9 (2½"-wide) strips. From strips, cut 144 (2½") H squares.

From dark red print, cut:
- 3 (4½"-wide) strips. From strips, cut 18 (4½") G squares.
- 8 C.

From dark blue print, cut:
- 3 (4½"-wide) strips. From strips, cut 18 (4½") G squares.
- 7 (2¼"-wide) strips for binding.
- 8 E.

Center Assembly

1. Referring to *Appliqué Placement Diagram*, lay out appliqué pieces on cream print background square. Fuse in place.

Sew Smart™

Fold and lightly press background square into quadrants and then in half diagonally. Use fold lines for accurate placement of appliqué pieces (*Appliqué Placement Diagram*).
—Marianne

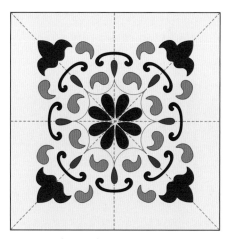

Appliqué Placement Diagram

2. Using matching thread, zigzag stitch around appliqué pieces.

3. Referring to *Quilt Top Assembly Diagram*, mark lines connecting dark blue E pieces using Marking Template on page 69. Using dark blue pearl cotton, stem stitch on lines *(Stem Stitch Diagram)*.

Stem Stitch Diagram

Block Assembly

1. Referring to *Diagonal Seams Diagrams*, place 1 cream print H square atop 1 dark blue print G square, right sides facing. Stitch diagonally from corner to corner as shown. Trim ¼" beyond stitching. Press open to reveal triangle. Repeat for 3 remaining corners to complete 1 blue Square-in-a-Square Unit. Make 18 blue Square-in-a-Square Units.

Diagonal Seams Diagrams

2. In the same manner, make 18 red Square-in-a-Square Units using cream print H squares and dark red print G squares.

3. Lay out 2 cream print G squares, 1 red Square-in-a-Square Unit and 1 blue Square-in-a-Square Unit as shown in *Block Assembly Diagram*. Join to complete 1 block *(Block Diagram)*. Make 18 blocks.

Block Assembly Diagram

Block Diagram

Quilt Assembly

1. Lay out center unit, F squares, and blocks as shown in *Quilt Top Assembly Diagram*.

2. Join into rows; join rows to complete quilt top.

Finishing

1. Divide backing into 2 (1¾-yard) lengths. Join panels lengthwise. Seam will run horizontally.

2. Layer backing, batting, and quilt top; baste. Quilt as desired. Quilt shown was outline quilted around appliqué and has an allover swirl design in the red and blue A squares and cream print background *(Quilting Diagram)*.

3. Join 2¼"-wide dark blue print strips into 1 continuous piece for straight-grain French-fold binding. Add binding to quilt.

Quilting Diagram

Quilt Top Assembly Diagram

C

A

Patterns are shown full size
for use with fusible web. Add $^3/_{16}$"
seam allowance for hand appliqué

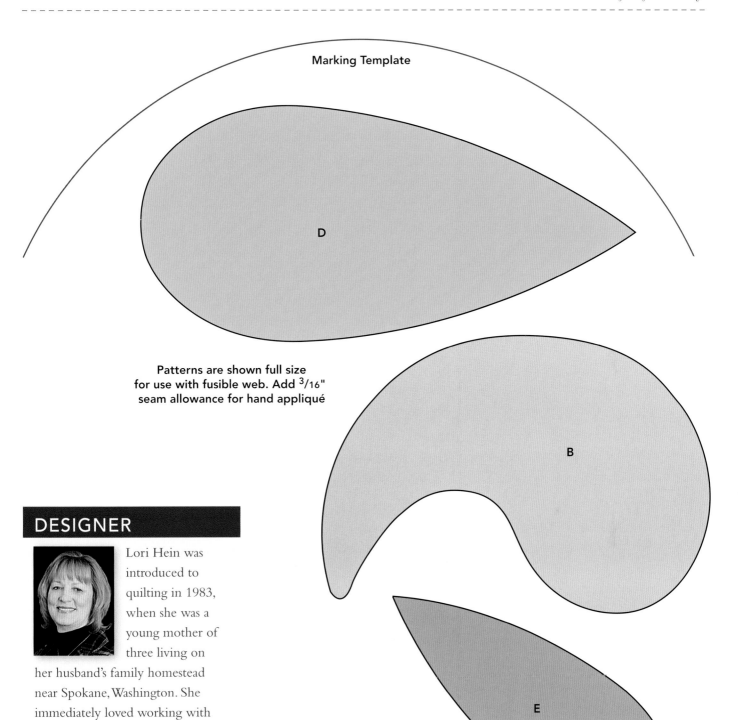

Marking Template

D

Patterns are shown full size
for use with fusible web. Add $^3/_{16}$"
seam allowance for hand appliqué

B

E

DESIGNER

Lori Hein was
introduced to
quilting in 1983,
when she was a
young mother of
three living on
her husband's family homestead
near Spokane, Washington. She
immediately loved working with
the fabrics and block designs. When
her children were nearly raised,
Lori began working at a quilt shop,
teaching classes, and designing her
own quilt patterns. In 2005, she
launched her Web site company,
Cool Water Quilts.

Contact her at:

lori@coolwaterquilts.com

www.coolwaterquilts.com ☀

Liberty

Designer Pam Kuehl combined her love of patriotic quilts and small projects to design this delightful miniature quilt. Because you use pre-printed flags, you can start this one on July 3rd and have it ready to display on Independence Day!

PROJECT RATING: EASY

Size: 15½" × 15½"

MATERIALS

4 pre-printed flags that are about
4" × 7" finished size

¾ yard red-and-cream toile print
for setting, backing, and binding

4" square navy solid for star

Paper-backed fusible web

18" square quilt batting

Cutting

Measurements include ¼" seam allowances. Follow manufacturer's instructions
for using fusible web.

From red-and-cream toile print, cut:

• 2 (2¼"-wide) strips for binding.

• 1 (18") square for quilt back.

• 1 (11½") square. Cut square in half
diagonally in both directions to make
4 side setting triangles.
NOTE: Triangles are oversized.

• 1 (4½") center square.

• 2 (4") squares. Cut squares in half
diagonally to make 4 corner setting
triangles. **NOTE:** Triangles are
oversized.

From navy, cut:

• 1 Star.

Assembly

1. Position Star on center square; fuse
in place. Hand or machine blanket
stitch around star *(Blanket Stitch
Diagram).*

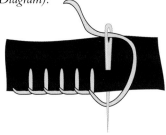

Blanket Stitch Diagram

2. Lay out flags, setting triangles, and
center square as shown in *Quilt Top
Assembly Diagram.*

Quilt Top Assembly Diagram

3. Join in diagonal rows; join rows. Use
large square ruler to square up quilt
top, leaving at least ¼" beyond corners
of flags for seam allowance.

Quilting and Finishing

1. Layer backing, batting, and quilt top;
baste. Quilt as desired. Quilt shown
was quilted in the ditch along all
seams and along flag fields. The star
appliqué shape was used as a quilting
design template for large setting
triangles.

2. Join 2¼"-wide toile strips into 1
continuous piece for straight-grain
French-fold binding. Add binding to
quilt.

DESIGNER

Pam Kuehl has
been quilting for
more than twenty-
five years. She
loves designing
quilts and teaching
her projects at over a dozen retreats
she organizes each year. ✳

Star

**Pattern is shown full size
for use with fusible web. Add ³/16"
seam allowance for hand appliqué**

Banner Day

Decorate your picnic table with this patriotic runner. The center square only looks appliquéd—a pre-printed panel saves sewing time.

PROJECT RATING: EASY
Size: 28" × 68"
Blocks: 4 (12") Star blocks

MATERIALS

¾ yard banner print
1 fat quarter* each gold print and red print
½ yard tan print
¾ yards blue ticking stripe
⅜ yard red ticking stripe
1 yard navy print
2 yards backing fabric
Twin-size quilt batting
*fat quarter = 18" × 20"

Cutting

Measurements include ¼" seam allowances. Border strips are exact length needed. You may want to make them longer to allow for piecing variations.

From banner print, cut:
• 1 (20½") square, centering design.

From gold print fat quarter, cut:
• 2 (6⅛"-wide) strips. From strips, cut 4 (6⅛") A squares.

From red print fat quarter, cut:
• 3 (5¼"-wide) strips. From strips, cut 8 (5¼") squares. Cut squares in half diagonally in both directions to make 32 quarter-square B triangles.

From tan print, cut:
• 1 (5¼"-wide) strip. From strip, cut 4 (5¼") squares. Cut squares in half diagonally in both directions to make 16 quarter-square B triangles.
• 2 (4½"-wide) strips. From strips, cut 16 (4½") C squares.

From blue ticking stripe, cut:
• 3 (2½"-wide) strips. From strips, cut 46 (2½") D squares.
• 6 (2¼"-wide) strips for binding.

From red ticking stripe, cut:
• 3 (2½"-wide) strips. From strips, cut 46 (2½") D squares.

From navy print, cut:
• 10 (2½"-wide) strips. From strips, cut 6 (2½" × 24½") E rectangles. Piece remaining strips to make 2 (2½" × 68½") side border strips.

Block Assembly

1. Join 1 tan print C square and 2 red print B triangles as shown in *Corner Unit Diagrams*. Make 16 Corner Units.

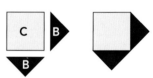

Corner Unit Diagrams

2. Lay out 1 gold print A square, 4 Corner Units, and 4 tan print B triangles as shown in *Block Assembly Diagram*. Join into diagonal rows; join rows to complete 1 Star block (*Block Diagram*). Make 4 Star blocks.

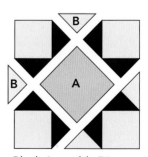

Block Assembly Diagram

Block Diagram

Row Assembly

1. Join 6 blue stripe D squares and 6 red stripe D squares to make 1 long row *(Long Row Diagram)*. Make 6 long rows.

> ### Sew **Smart**™
> Pay attention to direction of stripes in long and short stripe rows.
> —Marianne

D

Long Row Diagram

2. In the same manner, join 5 red stripe D squares and 5 blue stripe D squares to make 1 short row *(Short Row Diagram)*. Make 2 short rows.

D

Short Row Diagram

Quilt Assembly

1. Lay out center square, short and long rows, Star blocks, and navy E rectangles as shown in *Quilt Top Assembly Diagram*. Join into rows; join rows to complete table runner center.

2. Add navy side borders to table runner center.

Finishing

1. Divide backing into 2 (1-yard) lengths. Join panels end to end. Seam will run horizontally.

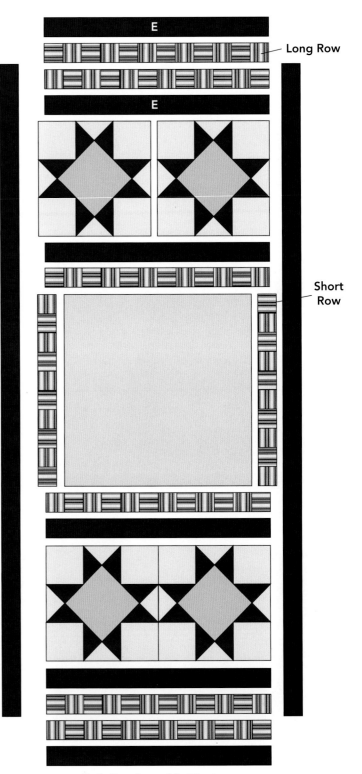

Quilt Top Assembly Diagram

2. Layer backing, batting, and quilt top; baste. Quilt as desired. Quilt shown was quilted in the ditch and around motifs in center, and has star and meandering design in blocks *(Quilting Diagram)*.

3. Join 2¼"-wide blue stripe strips into 1 continuous piece for straight-grain French-fold binding. Add binding to quilt.

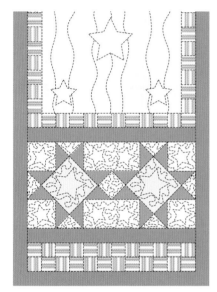

Quilting Diagram

DESIGNER

Jean Ann Wright has been a professional quiltmaker for many years. She is an editor in the quilting industry, and designs quilts for several fabric manufacturers and a thread company. Jean Ann indulges her artistic side by designing and creating art quilts and experimenting with surface design and thread play.

Contact her at:

www.jeanannquilts.com ✳

Valiant Eagle

Marianne Fons used reproduction prints to make this quilt for the
Quilts of Valor Foundation, which gives quilts to soldiers. She used the eagle pattern
from the antique *Flying Eagles* quilt on page 82.

PROJECT RATING: INTERMEDIATE

Size: 64" × 80"

Blocks: 28 (8") Variable Star blocks

8 (4") Pinwheel blocks

MATERIALS

⅝ yard cream solid

1 fat eighth★ red print for head

1 fat quarter★★ light gold print for
shield and pinwheels

3 fat quarters★★ assorted red prints
for stars

⅜ yard dark blue print for wings
and stripes

½ yard medium blue print for stars
and stripes

1 fat quarter★★ light blue print for
tail and stripes

½ yard yellow print for quilt center

½ yard green print for stars and
pinwheels

⅜ yard dark gold print for stars and
talons

1 yard dark shirting print for stars

⅞ yard light shirting print #1 for
stars and stripes

⅝ yard light shirting print #2 for
stars

1¼ yards red stripe for stars, border
#2, and binding

1⅝ yards black print

9" × 10" rectangle black solid or 24"
of pre-folded ½"-wide bias tape

5 yards backing fabric

Twin-size quilt batting

★fat eighth = 9" × 20"

★★fat quarter = 18" × 20"

Cutting

Measurements include ¼" seam
allowances. Border strips are exact
length needed. You may want to make
them longer to allow for piecing
variations. Patterns for appliqué are on
pages 84–87. Follow manufacturer's
instructions for using fusible web.

From cream solid, cut:

• 1 (19⅝") background square.

From red print fat eighth, cut:

• 1 Head.

From light gold print fat quarter, cut:

• 2 (2⅞"-wide) strips. From strips, cut
8 (2⅞") squares. Cut squares in half
diagonally to make 16 half-square A
triangles.

• 1 Shield.

From each red print fat quarter, cut:

• 2 (4½"-wide) strips. From strips, cut 7
(4½") D squares.

From dark blue print, cut:

• 2 (2½"-wide) strips. From strips, cut 6
(2½" × 8½") E rectangles.

• 1 Wing.

• 1 Wing reversed.

From medium blue print, cut:

• 5 (2½"-wide) strips. From strips, cut
6 (2½" × 8½") E rectangles and 56
(2½") C squares.

From light blue print fat quarter, cut:

• 4 (2½"-wide) strips. From strips, cut 8 (2½" × 8½") E rectangles.

• 1 Tail.

• 4 (3") G squares.

From yellow print, cut:

• 1 (14⅜"-wide) strip. From strip, cut 2 (14⅜") squares. Cut squares in half diagonally to make 4 half-square H triangles.

From green print, cut:

• 1 (2⅞"-wide) strip. From strip, cut 8 (2⅞") squares. Cut squares in half diagonally to make 16 half-square A triangles.

• 4 (2½"-wide) strips. From strips, cut 56 (2½") C squares.

From dark gold print, cut:

• 4 (2½"-wide) strips. From strips, cut 56 (2½") C squares.

• 2 Talons.

From dark shirting print, cut:

• 1 (2⅞"-wide) strip. From strip, cut 8 (2⅞") squares. Cut squares in half diagonally to make 16 half-square A triangles.

• 11 (2½"-wide) strips. From strips, cut 56 (2½" × 4½") B rectangles and 56 (2½") C squares.

From light shirting print #1, cut:

• 10 (2½"-wide) strips. From strips, cut 18 (2½" × 8½") E rectangles, 28 (2½" × 4½") B rectangles, and 28 (2½") C squares.

• 1 (1½"-wide) strip. From strip, cut 4 (1½" × 8½") F rectangles.

From light shirting print #2, cut:

• 1 (2⅞"-wide) strip. From strip, cut 8 (2⅞") squares. Cut squares in half diagonally to make 16 half-square A triangles.

• 6 (2½"-wide) strips. From strips, cut 28 (2½" × 4½") B rectangles and 28 (2½") C squares.

From red stripe, cut:

• 5 (4½"-wide) strips. From strips, cut 4 (4½" × 32½") border #2 and 7 (4½") D squares.

• 8 (2¼"-wide) strips for binding.

From black print, cut:

• 7 (4½"-wide) strips. Piece strips to make 2 (4½" × 72½") side border #4 and 2 (4½" × 56½") top and bottom border #4.

• 4 (3"-wide) strips. From strips, cut 4 (3" × 27½") border #1.

• 4 (2½"-wide) strips. From strips, cut 56 (2½") C squares.

From black solid, cut:

• 24" of bias strips.

 WEB EXTRA

To determine width of strips, download *Sew Easy: Making Bias* at www.FonsandPorter.com/makingbias.

OR 1 each letters U, S, and A from patterns on page 80.

• 1 Eye.

Quilt Center Assembly

1. Position Head, Eye, Tail, Wings, Talons, and Shield on cream solid background square as shown in *Quilt Center Diagram*. Fuse in place. Make letters as shown in *Sew Easy: Bias Letters* on page 81, or fuse letters. Machine appliqué using matching thread.

Quilt Center Diagram

2. Add yellow print H triangles to appliqué block to complete quilt center.

Block Assembly

1. Join 1 green print A triangle and 1 dark shirting print A triangle as shown in *Triangle-Square Diagrams*. Make 16 dark triangle-squares. In the same manner, make 16 light triangle-squares, using light gold print and light shirting print #2 A triangles.

MAKE 16   MAKE 16

Triangle-Square Diagrams

2. Lay out 4 dark triangle-squares as shown in *Pinwheel Block Diagrams*. Join into rows; join rows to complete 1 dark Pinwheel block. Make 4 dark Pinwheel blocks and 4 light Pinwheel blocks.

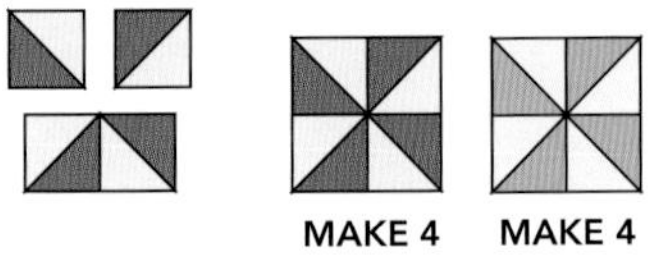

MAKE 4   MAKE 4

Pinwheel Block Diagrams

3. Referring to *Star Point Unit Diagrams*, place 1 green print C square atop 1 dark shirting print B rectangle, right sides facing. Stitch diagonally from corner to corner as shown. Trim ¼" beyond stitching. Press open to reveal triangle. Repeat for opposite end of rectangle to complete 1 Star Point Unit. Make 4 green Star Point Units.

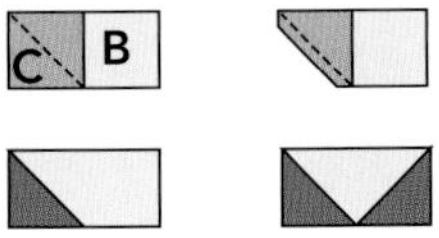

Star Point Unit Diagrams

4. Lay out 1 red print D square, 4 green Star Point Units, and 4 dark shirting print C squares as shown in *Star Block Assembly Diagram*. Join into rows; join rows to complete 1 dark Star block *(Star Block Diagram)*. Make 14 dark Star blocks using black, green, medium blue, and gold for star points and dark shirting print for background.

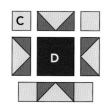

Star Block Assembly Diagram

Star Block Diagram

5. In the same manner, make 14 light Star blocks using remaining black, green, medium blue, and dark gold for star points and light shirting print #1 or #2 for background.

Star Border Assembly

1. Lay out 4 dark Star blocks and 3 light Star blocks as shown in *Quilt Top Assembly Diagram*. Join to complete 1 side Star Border. Make 2 side Star borders.

2. In a similar manner, lay out 4 light Star blocks and 3 dark Star blocks. Join to complete top Star border. Repeat for bottom Star border.

Stripe Section Assembly

1. Lay out 9 light shirting print #1 E rectangles, 2 light shirting print #1 F rectangles, 3 dark blue print

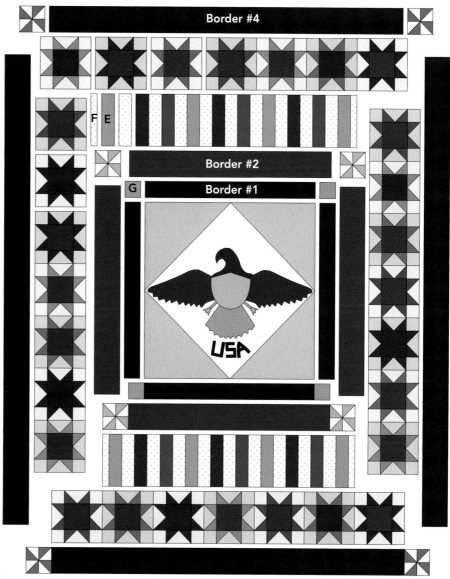

Quilt Top Assembly Diagram

E rectangles, 3 medium blue print E rectangles, and 4 light blue print E rectangles as shown in *Quilt Top Assembly Diagram*.

2. Join to complete 1 stripe section. Make 2 stripe sections.

Quilt Assembly

1. Referring to *Quilt Top Assembly Diagram*, add black print border #1 to sides of quilt center. Add 1 light blue print G square to each end of remaining black print borders. Add borders to top and bottom of quilt.

2. Add red stripe side border #2 to quilt center. Add 1 light pinwheel block to each end of remaining red stripe borders. Add borders to top and bottom of quilt.

3. Add stripe sections to top and bottom of quilt.

4. Add side Star borders to quilt center. Add top and bottom Star borders to quilt.

5. Add black print side border #4 to quilt center. Add 1 dark pinwheel block to each end of top and bottom border #4. Add borders to quilt.

Finishing

1. Divide backing into 2 (2½-yard) lengths. Cut 1 piece in half lengthwise to make 2 narrow panels. Join 1 narrow panel to each side of wider panel; press seam allowances toward narrow panels.

2. Layer backing, batting, and quilt top; baste. Quilt as desired. Quilt shown was quilted with meandering in appliqué block, rays in yellow triangles, in the ditch around stars and stripes, with Xs in red stripe border, and with parallel lines in black outer border *(Quilting Diagram)*.

3. Join 2¼"-wide red stripe strips into 1 continuous piece for straight-grain French-fold binding. Add binding to quilt. ✳

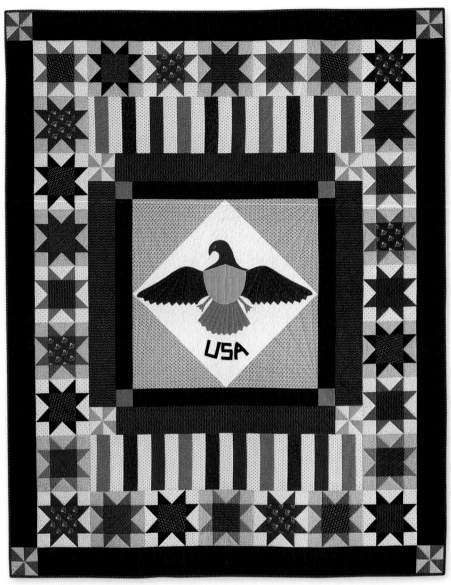

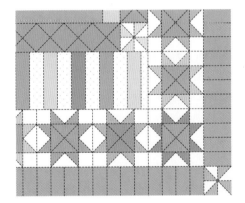

Quilting Diagram

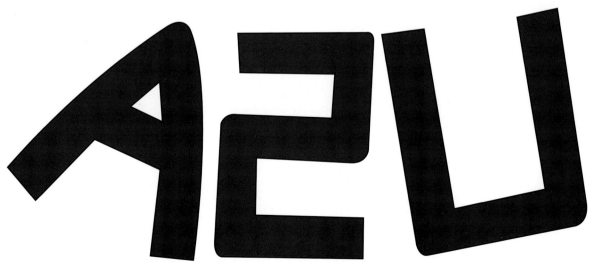

Patterns are shown full size and are reversed for use with fusible web. Add $^{3}/_{16}$" seam allowance for hand appliqué

Bias Letters

Use this quick and easy method to make letters from bias strips.

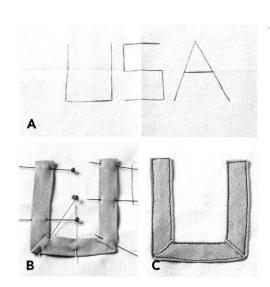

A

B

C

1. Prepare bias strips or use pre-packaged bias tape.
2. Using pencil, draw letters on background fabric *(Photo A)*.
3. Turn under seam allowance on beginning end of strip, and pin strip to background fabric, centering strip over line. Fold strip at corners to make miters *(Photo B)*. Turn under finishing end.
4. Topstitch along edges of letter and on mitered corners *(Photo C)*.

Flying Eagles

This wonderful antique quilt is from the collection of the International Quilt Study Center & Museum in Lincoln, Nebraska. You can hand appliqué your quilt as the original maker did, or speed up construction using machine appliqué.

QUILT FROM THE COLLECTION OF **International Quilt Study Center & Museum 1997.007.0126.**

PROJECT RATING: INTERMEDIATE

Size: 77" × 77"

Blocks: 9 (20") Eagle blocks

MATERIALS

5⅞ yards white solid

2¼ yards green print

¾ yard red solid

1 yard brown solid

Paper-backed fusible web

4¾ yards backing fabric

Full-size quilt batting

Cutting

Measurements include ¼" seam allowances. Border strips are exact length needed. You may want to make them longer to allow for piecing variations. Appliqué patterns are on pages 84–87. Follow manufacturer's instructions for using fusible web.

From white, cut:

• 9 (2¼"-wide) strips for binding.

• 1 (20½"-wide) **lengthwise** strip. From strip, cut 9 (20½") squares.

• 2 (9"-wide) **lengthwise** strips. From strips, cut 2 (9" × 77½") top and bottom borders and 2 (9" × 60½") side borders.

From green, cut:

• 9 Large Wings.

• 9 Large Wings reversed.

• 9 Large Tails.

• 24 Small Wings.

• 24 Small Wings reversed.

• 24 Small Tails.

From red, cut:

• 9 Large Heads.

• 24 Small Heads.

• 18 Legs.

From brown, cut:

• 9 Large Shields.

• 24 Small Shields.

• 18 Talons.

• 9 Large Eyes.

• 24 Small Eyes.

Quilt Assembly

1. Position 2 Large Wings, 2 Legs, 2 Talons, 1 Large Tail, 1 Large Head, 1 Large Shield, and 1 Large Eye on 1 white background square as shown in *Eagle Block Diagram.*

Eagle Block Diagram

2. Fuse pieces in place; machine appliqué using matching thread to complete 1 block. Make 9 blocks.

3. Lay out blocks as shown in *Quilt Top Assembly Diagram* on page 84. Join into rows; join rows to complete quilt center.

Border Assembly

1. Fold 1 side border in half crosswise; crease to mark center. Place 2 Small Wings, 1 Small Tail, 1 Small Head, 1 Small Shield, and 1 Small Eye atop border, centering pieces on crease; fuse in place. Place pieces for 4 more small eagles on border, evenly spacing them as shown in *Quilt Top Assembly Diagram.* Fuse pieces in place.

> **Sew Smart**™
>
> To position eagles on borders, lay border strips beside quilt center to help with placement. —Liz

2. Machine appliqué pieces to border strip to complete 1 side border. Make 2 side borders. Add side borders to quilt center.

3. In the same manner, appliqué 7 small eagles on top border. Repeat for bottom border. Add top and bottom borders to quilt.

Finishing

1. Divide backing into 2 (2⅜-yard) lengths. Cut 1 piece in half lengthwise to make 2 narrow panels. Join 1 narrow panel to each side of wider panel; press seam allowances toward narrow panels.

2. Layer backing, batting, and quilt top; baste. Quilt as desired. Quilt shown was quilted with feathers in background and parallel lines on eagles (*Quilting Diagram*).

3. Join 2¼"-wide white strips into 1 continuous piece for straight-grain French-fold binding. Add binding to quilt.

Quilting Diagram

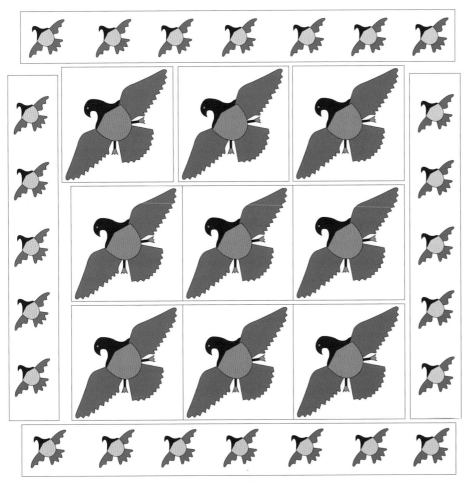

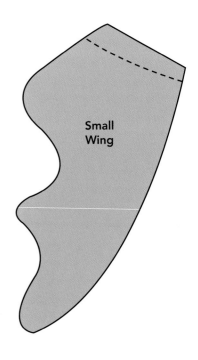

Small Wing

Quilt Top Assembly Diagram

From the Curator—

Nine large and twenty-four small eagles fly in formation across this circa 1870–1890 quilt, which measures 77" × 73". The unknown maker was possibly from rural Cherry Tree Township in western Pennsylvania. Quilt collector, dealer, curator, and author Roderick Kiracofe notes that most examples of eagle quilts have a Pennsylvania origin. This leads to the speculation that the pattern was shared or copied among a regional group of quilters.

The brown, green, and red appliquéd eagles in the center of the quilt are set on the diagonal. Flowing lines of quilted feather plumes in the white background mimic air currents sweeping around them as they fly through the sky. "The brown fabric used in the eagle's shield is fading unevenly throughout the quilt," says Carolyn Ducey, Curator of Collections at the International Quilt Study Center & Museum. "This may be due to an uneven dye process or the use of a fugitive dye that is slowly losing its color."

In 1782, Congress adopted the American bald eagle for the Great Seal, serving as a symbol of liberty, loyalty, and patriotism. During the Civil War years, 1861–1865, northern quilters made Union quilts with eagles and stars, and the greatest number of these were made in Pennsylvania. "When Americans celebrated the centennial of our country in 1876, many women put appliquéd eagles on their quilts to commemorate the important date," says Ms. Ducey. The eagle was also a popular motif on Baltimore album quilts well into the twentieth century.

About the Collection: In each issue, *Love of Quilting* features an antique quilt and pattern from the International Quilt Study Center & Museum at the University of Nebraska-Lincoln. The Center has the largest publicly held quilt collection in the world. See other gorgeous quilts from the collection and enjoy interactive Web features at www.quiltstudy.org under Quilt Explorer. ❋

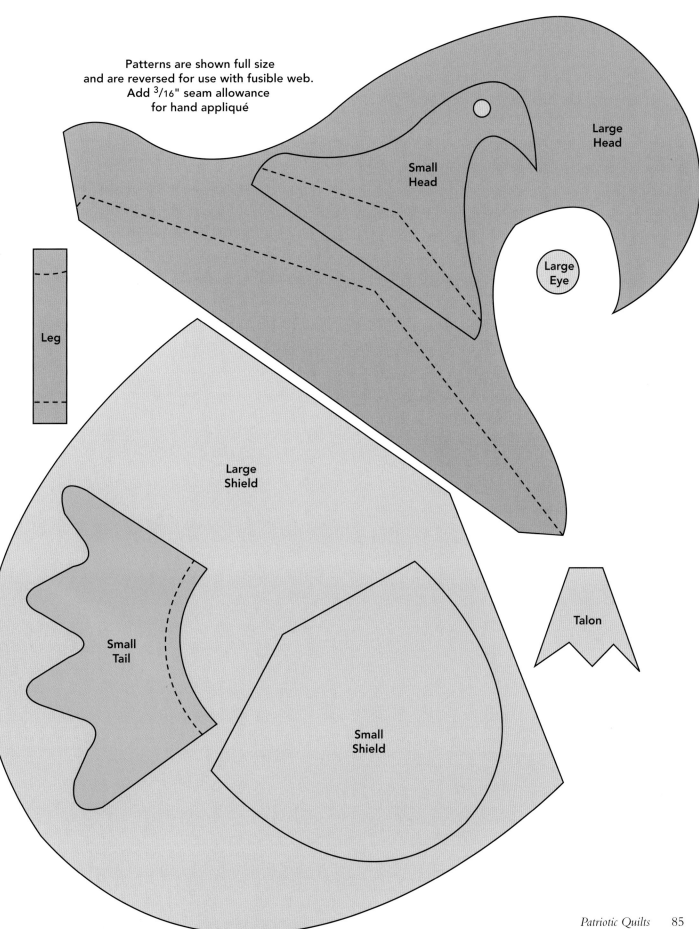

Patterns are shown full size
and are reversed for use with fusible web.
Add $^3/_{16}$" seam allowance
for hand appliqué

Large
Head

Small
Head

Large
Eye

Leg

Large
Shield

Small
Tail

Small
Shield

Talon

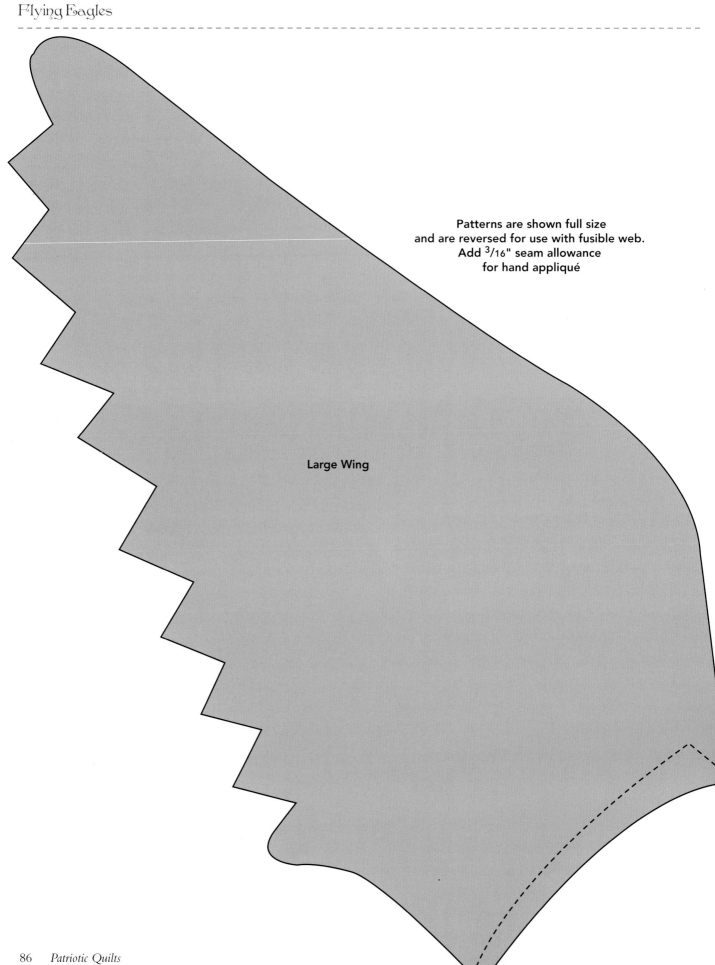

Patterns are shown full size
and are reversed for use with fusible web.
Add $^3/_{16}$" seam allowance
for hand appliqué

Large Wing

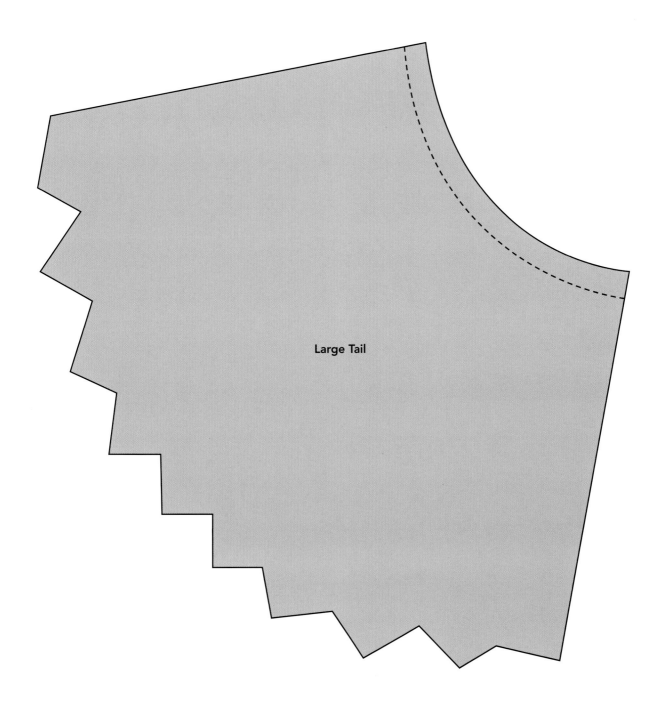

Large Tail

Primarily Stars

Jodie Davis of QNNtv designed this scrappy star quilt. At first glance you see red stars, but careful color placement makes a secondary blue star pattern appear.

Size: 63" × 81"
Blocks: 12 (18") Star blocks

MATERIALS

12 fat eighths★★ assorted
   green prints
8 fat quarters★ assorted red prints
6 fat eighths★★ assorted
   blue prints
6 fat quarters★ assorted
   yellow prints
9 fat quarters★ assorted tan prints
½ yard blue print for inner border
¾ yard red print for binding
Fons & Porter Half & Quarter
   Ruler (optional)
5 yards backing fabric
Twin-size quilt batting
★fat quarter = 18" × 20"
★★fat eighth = 9" × 20"

Cutting

Measurements include ¼" seam allowances. Border strips are exact length needed. You may want to make them longer to allow for piecing variations.

 WEB EXTRA
To cut triangles for triangle-squares using the Fons & Porter Half & Quarter Ruler, download *Sew Easy: Cutting Half-Square Triangles* at www.FonsandPorter.com/chst. If you are not using the Fons & Porter Half & Quarter Ruler, use the cutting **NOTE** instructions given here.

From each green print fat eighth, cut:
• 1 (6½"-wide) strip. From strip, cut 1 (6½") A square.

From red print fat quarters, cut a total of:
• 19 (3½"-wide) strips. From strips, cut 92 (3½") B squares.
• 12 (3½"-wide) strips. From strips, cut 96 half-square D triangles.
   NOTE: If NOT using the Fons & Porter Half & Quarter Ruler to cut the D triangles, cut 12 (3⅞"-wide) strips. From strips, cut 48 (3⅞") squares. Cut squares in half diagonally to make 96 half-square D triangles.

From each blue print fat eighth, cut:
• 2 (3½"-wide) strips. From strips, cut 16 half-square D triangles.
   NOTE: If NOT using the Fons & Porter Half & Quarter Ruler to cut the

D triangles, cut 2 (3⅞"-wide) strips. From strips, cut 8 (3⅞") squares. Cut squares in half diagonally to make 16 half-square D triangles.

From each yellow print fat quarter, cut:
• 4 (3½"-wide) strips. From strips, cut 32 half-square D triangles.
   NOTE: If NOT using the Fons & Porter Half & Quarter Ruler to cut the D triangles, cut 4 (3⅞"-wide) strips. From strips, cut 16 (3⅞") squares. Cut squares in half diagonally to make 32 half-square D triangles.

From tan print fat quarters, cut a total of:
• 10 (6½"-wide) strips. From strips, cut 48 (6½" × 3½") C rectangles.
• 20 (3½"-wide) strips. From strips, cut 96 (3½") B squares.

From blue print, cut:
• 7 (2"-wide) strips. Piece strips to make 2 (2" × 72½") side inner borders and 2 (2" × 57½") top and bottom inner borders.

From red print, cut:
• 8 (2¼"-wide) strips for binding.

Block Assembly

1. Join 1 yellow print D triangle and 1 blue print D triangle as shown in *Triangle-Square Diagrams*. Make 96 yellow/blue triangle-squares.

Triangle-Square Diagrams

2. In the same manner, make 96 yellow/red triangle-squares using yellow print and red print D triangles.

3. Lay out 8 tan print B squares, 4 tan print C rectangles, 8 assorted yellow/blue triangle-squares, 8 assorted yellow/red triangle-squares, and 1 green print A square as shown in *Block Assembly Diagram*. Join into rows; join rows to complete 1 Star block *(Block Diagram)*. Make 12 blocks.

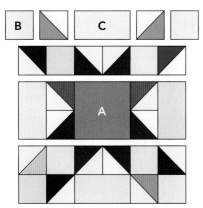

Block Assembly Diagram

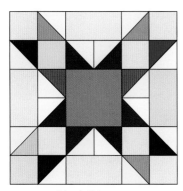

Block Diagram

Quilt Top Assembly Diagram

Quilt Assembly

1. Lay out blocks as shown in *Quilt Top Assembly Diagram*. Join into rows; join rows to complete quilt center.

2. Add blue print side inner borders to quilt center. Add top and bottom inner borders to quilt.

3. Join 25 assorted red print B squares to make 1 pieced side outer border. Make 2 pieced side outer borders. Add borders to quilt.

4. Join 21 assorted red print B squares to make pieced top outer border. Repeat for pieced bottom outer border. Add borders to quilt.

Finishing

1. Divide backing into 2 (2½-yard) lengths. Cut 1 piece in half lengthwise to make 2 narrow panels. Join 1 narrow panel to each side of wider panel; press seam allowances toward narrow panels.

2. Layer backing, batting, and quilt top; baste. Quilt as desired. Quilt shown was quilted with stars and swirls *(Quilting Diagram)*.

3. Join 2¼"-wide red print strips into 1 continuous piece for straight-grain French-fold binding. Add binding to quilt.

Quilting Diagram

TRIED & TRUE

Assorted blue-and-white prints are perfect for a two-color quilt. Fabrics shown are from the Cambridge Square collection by Northcott.

SIZE OPTIONS

	Crib (45" × 45")	Full (81" × 99")	Queen (99" × 117")
Blocks	4	20	30
Setting	2 × 2	4 × 5	5 × 6

MATERIALS

	Crib	Full	Queen
Green Prints	4 fat eighths	5 fat quarters	8 fat quarters
Red Prints	4 fat quarters	12 fat quarters	15 fat quarters
Blue Prints	2 fat eighths	5 fat quarters	8 fat quarters
Yellow Prints	2 fat quarters	10 fat quarters	15 fat quarters
Tan Prints	4 fat quarters	14 fat quarters	20 fat quarters
Blue Print	⅜ yard	⅝ yard	¾ yard
Red Print	½ yard	¾ yard	1 yard
Backing Fabric	1½ yards	7½ yards	9 yards
Batting	Twin-size	Queen-size	King-size

WEB EXTRA

Go to www.FonsandPorter.com/primarilysizes to download *Quilt Top Assembly Diagrams* for these size options.

DESIGNER

Jodie Davis loves paper piecing, but admits that not all quilts call for this technique. Once in awhile she likes to practice her traditional piecing skills while making scrappy stash-busting quilts. Jodie has a busy schedule as host of "Quilt Out Loud" and "Quilt It! The Longarm Quilting Show" on QNNtv.com.
Contact her at: www.QNNtv.com ✳

Stars and Stripes

Decorate your home for the Fourth of July by draping this patriotic quilt over a chair, or take it along for a sunny picnic. Use country colors, like the version shown here, or try bright novelty prints to really add fireworks.

Finished Size: 68¼" × 92½"
Blocks: 3 (24⅜" × 16¼") Flag Blocks

MATERIALS

18 (9") blue print squares for blocks
18 (9") light print squares for blocks
⅜ yard blue print #1 for star field
2⅜ yards blue print #2 for borders
¾ yard red print #1 for flag stripes
¾ yard red print #2 for binding
½ yard cream print #1 for flag stripes
½ yard cream print #2 for border
¼ yard gold print for stars
Fons & Porter Quarter Inch Seam Marker (optional)
Paper-backed fusible web
5½ yards backing fabric
Twin-size quilt batting

Cutting

Measurements include ¼" seam allowances. Border strips are exact length needed. You may want to cut them longer to allow for piecing variations. Star patterns are on pages 94 and 95.

Follow manufacturer's instructions for using fusible web.

From blue print #1, cut:
- 3 (8" × 10½") A rectangles.

From blue print #2, cut:
- 4 (2½"-wide) **lengthwise** strips. From strips, cut 2 (2½" × 73⅝") side inner borders and 2 (2½" × 53¼") top and bottom inner borders.
- 4 (6½"-wide) **lengthwise** strips. From strips, cut 2 (6½" × 81⅛") side outer borders and 2 (6½" × 68¾") top and bottom outer borders.

From red print #1, cut:
- 12 (1¾"-wide) strips. From strips, cut 12 (1¾" × 24⅞") C strips and 9 (1¾" × 14⅞") B strips.

From red print #2, cut:
- 9 (2¼"-wide) strips for binding.

From cream print #1, cut:
- 9 (1¾"-wide) strips. From strips, cut 9 (1¾" × 24⅞") C strips and 9 (1¾" × 14⅞") B strips.

From cream print #2, cut:
- 7 (2¼"-wide) strips. Piece strips to make 2 (2¼" × 77⅝") side middle borders and 2 (2¼" × 56¾") top and bottom middle borders.

From gold print:
- 3 Stars.

Flag Block Assembly

1. Referring to *Sew Easy: Quick Half-Square Triangle Units* on page 57, make 36 triangle-squares using blue print and light print 9" squares. **NOTE:** If not using the Fons & Porter Quarter Inch Seam Marker, cut blue print and light print 9" squares in half diagonally to make half-square triangles. Join 1 blue print half-square triangle and 1 light print half-square triangle to make a triangle-square. Make 36 triangle squares.

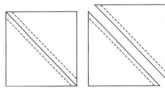

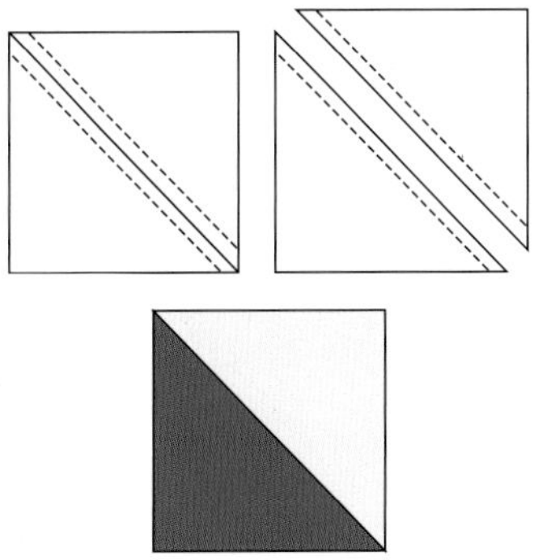

Triangle-Square Diagrams

2. Join 3 red print and 3 light print B strips as shown in *Block Assembly*

Diagram. Add 1 blue print A rectangle to left side to make upper section of flag. Join 4 red print and 3 light print C strips to make lower section of flag. Join sections to complete 1 Flag block *(Block Diagram).* Make 3 Flag blocks.

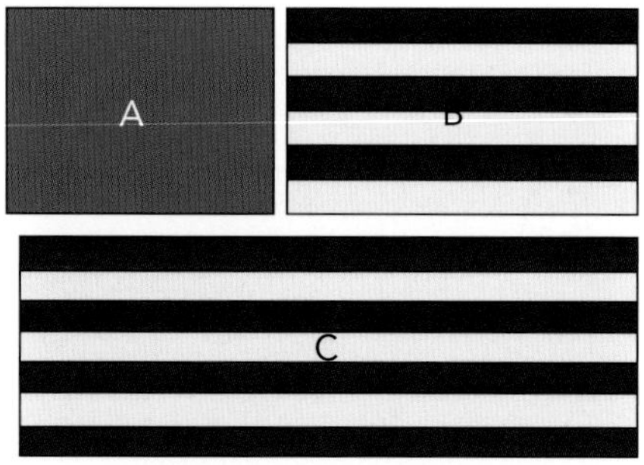

Block Assembly Diagram

Block Diagram

3. Position 1 gold print star atop each Flag block. Appliqué edges with blanket stitch *(Blanket Stitch Diagram).*

Quilt Assembly

1. Lay out triangle-squares and Flag blocks as shown in *Quilt Top Assembly Diagram.* Join triangle-squares into rows; join rows to make 3 sections. Join sections and Flag blocks to complete quilt center.

2. Add blue print #2 side inner borders to quilt center. Add top and bottom inner borders to quilt.

3. Repeat for cream print #2 middle borders and blue print #2 outer borders.

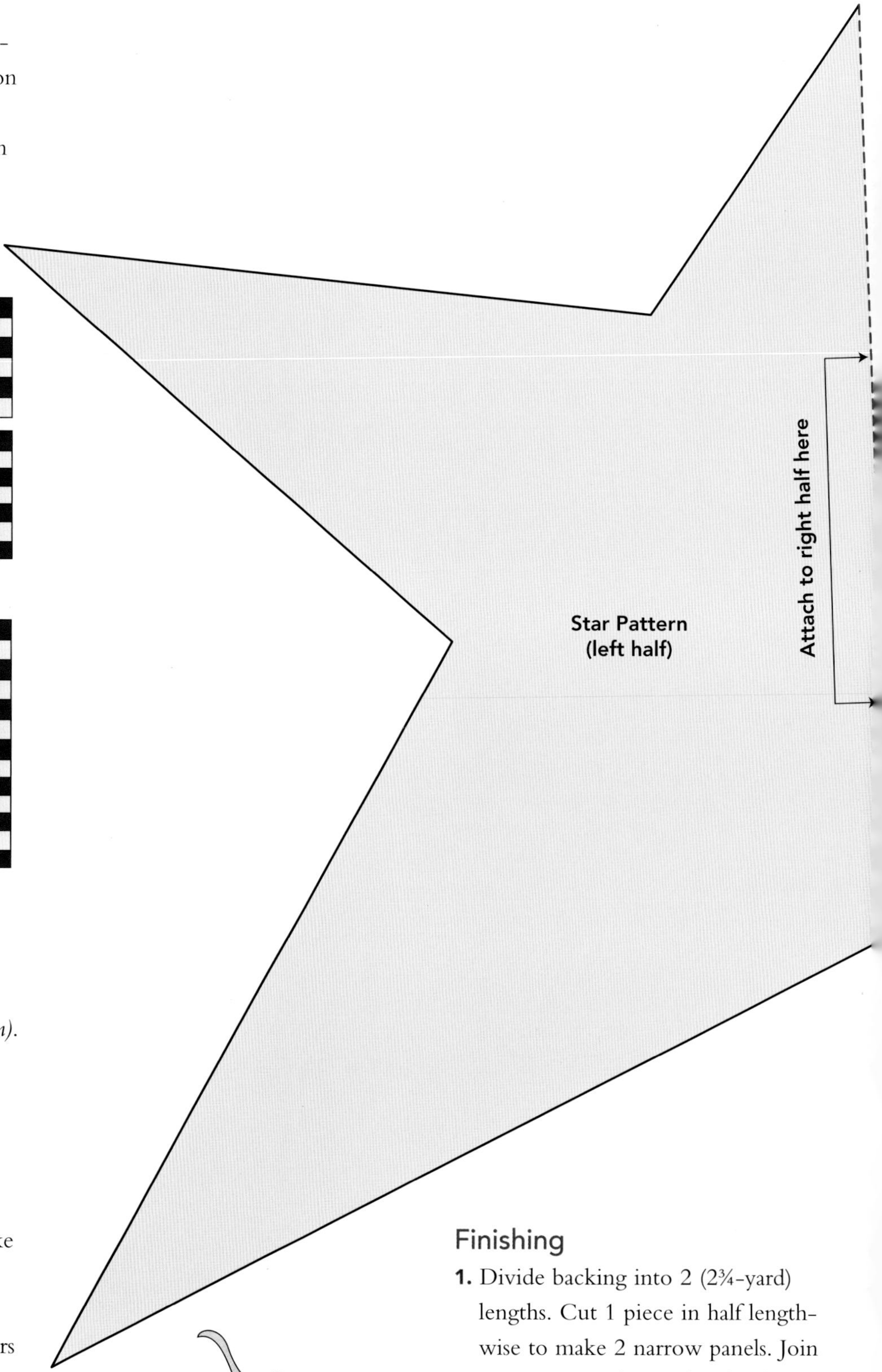

Star Pattern
(left half)

Attach to right half here

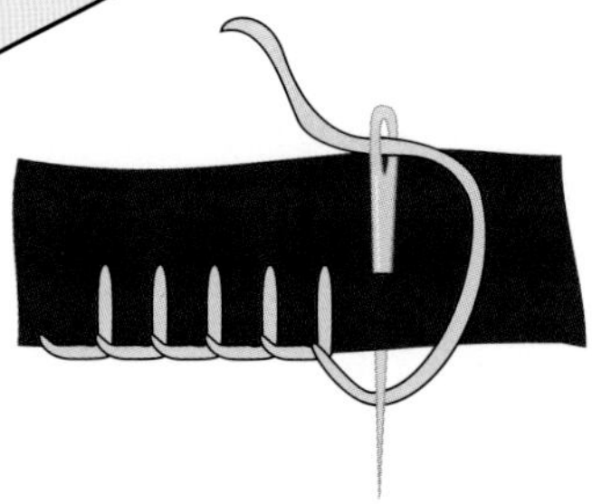

Blanket Stitch Diagram

Finishing

1. Divide backing into 2 (2¾-yard) lengths. Cut 1 piece in half lengthwise to make 2 narrow panels. Join 1 narrow panel to each side of wider panel; press seam allowances toward narrow panels.

2. Layer backing, batting, and quilt top; baste. Quilt as desired. Quilt shown was quilted with allover meandering.

Attach to left half here

Star Pattern (right half)

Quilt Top Assembly Diagram

3. Join 2¼"-wide red print #2 strips
into 1 continuous piece for straight-
grain French-fold binding. Add
binding to quilt.

QUILT BY **Rhoda Nelson**.
MACHINE QUILTED BY **Vicki Stratton**.

Beachfront Cottage

Fresh prints in vivid colors are just right for summer decorating.
Make triangle-squares for this quilt quickly using the Fons & Porter Quarter Inch
Seam Marker. See *Sew Easy: Quick Half-Square Triangle Units* on page 57.

PROJECT RATING: INTERMEDIATE
Size: 93" × 105"
Blocks: 42 (12") blocks

MATERIALS

3¾ yards cream print for
  background
4⅛ yards floral print for blocks,
  outer border, and binding
½ yard shell print for blocks
2 yards red print for blocks
1¾ yards dark blue print
  for blocks
⅝ yard medium blue print for
  middle border
⅞ yard stripe for inner border
Fons & Porter Quarter Inch Seam
  Marker (optional)
8¼ yards backing fabric
King-size quilt batting

Cutting

Measurements include ¼" seam allowances. Border strips are exact length needed. You may want to make them longer to allow for piecing variations.

From cream print, cut:

- 3 (5¼"-wide) strips. From strips, cut 21 (5¼") squares. Cut squares in half diagonally in both directions to make 84 quarter-square C triangles.
- 3 (4¼"-wide) strips. From strips, cut 21 (4¼") squares. Cut squares in half diagonally in both directions to make 84 quarter-square G triangles.
- 5 (3⅞"-wide) strips. From strips, cut 42 (3⅞") squares. Cut squares in half diagonally to make 84 half-square J triangles.
- 7 (2⅞"-wide) strips. From strips, cut 84 (2⅞") squares.
  NOTE: If not using the Fons & Porter Quarter Inch Seam Marker, cut squares in half diagonally to make 168 half-square D triangles.

- 11 (2⅝"-wide) strips for strip sets.
- 6 (2½"-wide) strips. From strips, cut 84 (2½") E squares.
- 6 (2⅜"-wide) strips. From strips, cut 84 (2⅜") squares. Cut squares in half diagonally to make 168 half-square H triangles.

From floral print, cut:

- 4 (6⅛"-wide) strips. From strips, cut 21 (6⅛") A squares.
- 11 (2¼"-wide) strips for binding.

From remainder of floral print, cut:

- 4 (7"-wide) **lengthwise** strips, centering red flowers on strips. From strips, cut 2 (7" × 93½") top and bottom outer borders and 2 (7" × 92½") side outer borders.

From shell print, cut:

- 3 (4¾"-wide) strips. From strips, cut 21 (4¾") F squares.

From red print, cut:

- 6 (4⅞"-wide) strips. From strips, cut 42 (4⅞") squares. Cut squares in half diagonally to make 84 half-square B triangles.

- 13 (2⅞"-wide) strips. From strips, cut 168 (2⅞") squares. Cut 84 squares in half diagonally to make 168 half-square D triangles.

  NOTE: If not using the Fons & Porter Quarter Inch Seam Marker, cut all 168 squares in half diagonally to make 336 half-square D triangles.

From dark blue print, cut:
- 4 (3"-wide) strips. From strips, cut 42 (3") squares. Cut squares in half diagonally to make 84 half-square I triangles.
- 11 (2⅝"-wide) strips for strip sets.
- 6 (2⅜"-wide) strips. From strips, cut 84 (2⅜") squares. Cut squares in half diagonally to make 168 half-square H triangles.

From medium blue print, cut:
- 9 (2"-wide) strips. Piece strips to make 2 (2" × 89½") side middle borders and 2 (2" × 80½") top and bottom middle borders.

From stripe, cut:
- 9 (3"-wide) strips. Piece strips to make 2 (3" × 84½") side inner borders and 2 (3" × 77½") top and bottom inner borders.

Block 1 Assembly

1. Lay out 1 floral print A square and 4 red print B triangles as shown in *Block Center Diagrams*. Join to complete 1 Block Center. Make 21 Block Centers.

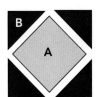

Block Center Diagrams

2. Join 1 cream print C triangle and 2 red print D triangles as shown in *Flying Geese Unit Diagrams*. Make 84 Flying Geese Units.

Flying Geese Diagrams

3. Referring to *Sew Easy: Quick Half-Square Triangle Units* on page 57, make 168 triangle-squares using 2⅞" cream print squares and 2⅞" red print squares. **NOTE:** If not using the Fons & Porter Quarter Inch Seam Marker, join 1 cream print D triangle and 1 red print D triangle to make a triangle-square. Make 168 triangle-squares.

4. Lay out 1 block center, 4 Flying Geese Units, 8 triangle-squares, and 4 cream print E squares as shown in *Block 1 Assembly Diagram*. Join into rows; join rows to complete 1 Block 1 *(Block 1 Diagram)*. Make 21 Block 1.

Block 1 Assembly Diagram

Block 1 Diagram

Block 2 Assembly

1. Join 1 cream print G triangle and 2 dark blue print H triangles to complete 1 Flying Geese Unit. Make 84 Flying Geese Units.

2. Lay out 1 Flying Geese Unit, 2 cream print H triangles, and 1 dark blue print I triangle as shown in *Side Unit Diagrams*. Join to complete 1 Side Unit. Make 84 Side Units.

Side Unit Diagrams

3. Join 1 (2⅝"-wide) cream print strip and 1 (2⅝"-wide) dark blue print strip as shown in *Strip Set Diagram*. Make 11 strip sets. From strip sets, cut 84 (4¾"-wide) segments.

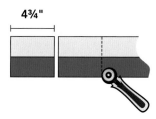

Strip Set Diagram

4. Lay out 1 shell print F square, 4 strip set segments, 4 Side Units, and 4 cream print J triangles as shown in *Block 2 Assembly Diagram*. Join into diagonal rows; join rows to complete 1 Block 2 *(Block 2 Diagram)*. Make 21 Block 2.

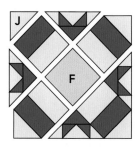

Block 2 Assembly Diagram

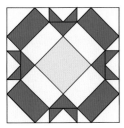

Block 2 Diagram

Quilt Assembly

1. Lay out blocks as shown in *Quilt Top Assembly Diagram*. Join into rows; join rows to complete quilt center.
2. Add stripe side inner borders to quilt center. Add stripe top and bottom inner borders to quilt.
3. Repeat for middle and outer borders.

Finishing

1. Divide backing into 3 (2¾-yard) lengths. Join panels lengthwise. Seams will run horizontally.
2. Layer backing, batting, and quilt top; baste. Quilt as desired. Quilt shown was quilted with an allover design *(Quilting Diagram)*.
3. Join 2¼"-wide floral print strips into 1 continuous piece for straight-grain French-fold binding. Add binding to quilt.

Quilt Top Assembly Diagram

Quilting Diagram

TRIED & TRUE

These refreshing, sherbet-colored prints from the Strawberry Field collection by Alice Kennedy for Timeless Treasures would make a beautiful summer quilt.

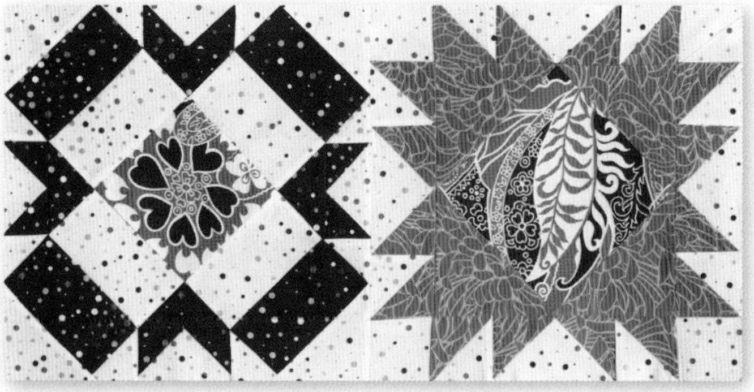

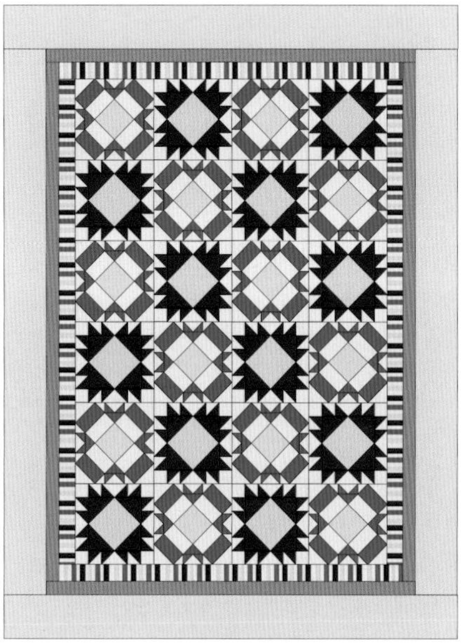

Twin

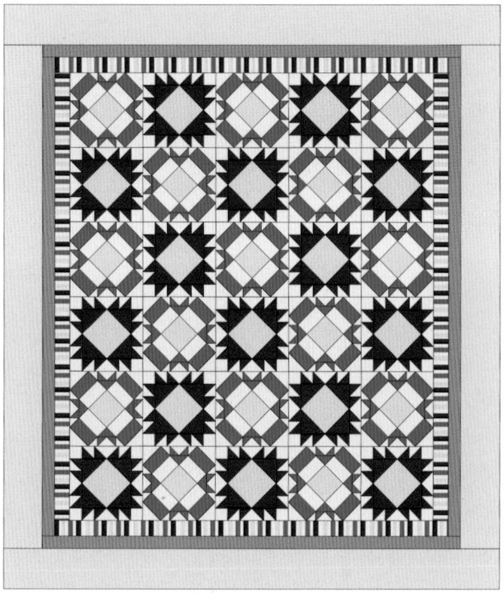

Full

SIZE OPTIONS

	Twin (69" × 93")	Full (81" × 93")
Block 1	12	15
Block 2	12	15
Setting	4 × 6	5 × 6

MATERIALS

Cream Print	2 yards	2⅜ yards
Floral Print	3¼ yards	3½ yards
Shell Print	⅜ yard	⅜ yard
Red Print	1¼ yards	1½ yards
Dark Blue Print	¾ yard	1 yard
Medium Blue Print	½ yard	⅝ yard
Stripe	¾ yard	¾ yard
Backing Fabric	5½ yards	7⅜ yards
Batting	Twin-size	Queen-size

DESIGNER

Rhoda Nelson is a professional quiltmaker and designer who creates original quilts to showcase new fabric designs.

Contact her at: Designs by Rhoda • www.dbrhoda.com ✳

Liberty Hall

Choose reproduction fabrics with a tea-dyed,
time-worn look for this easy patriotic quilt.

Size: 54" × 63"

Blocks: 32 (6") Nine Patch blocks

MATERIALS

¾ yard America fabric for quilt
center (or 18½" square of focal
print)

7 fat eighths★ assorted dark blue
prints

4 fat eighths★ assorted red prints

½ yard light print #1

½ yard light print #2

¼ yard light print #3 for letters

1½ yards blue print #1

1 fat eighth★ blue print #2 for stars

⅝ yard red print

¾ yard medium brown print for
blocks and binding

Paper-backed fusible web

3½ yards backing fabric

Twin-size quilt batting

★fat eighth = 9" × 20"

Cutting

Measurements include ¼" seam
allowances. Patterns for letters and
stars are on pages 106–107. Follow
manufacturer's instructions for using
fusible web.

From America fabric, cut:

• 1 (18½") square, centering medallion.

**From each dark blue print fat eighth,
cut:**

• 2 (2½"-wide) strips for strip sets.

From each red print fat eighth, cut:

• 3 (2½"-wide) strips. From 1 strip, cut
4 (2½") A squares. Remaining strips
are for strip sets.

From light print #1, cut:

• 6 (2½"-wide) strips. Cut 5 strips in
half to make 10 (2½" × 20") strips for
strip sets. From remaining strip, cut 8
(2½") A squares.

From light print #2, cut:

• 6 (2½"-wide) strips. Cut 5 strips in
half to make 10 (2½" × 20") strips for
strip sets. From remaining strip, cut 8
(2½") A squares.

From light print #3, cut:

• 1 each L, I, B, E, R, T, and Y.

From blue print #1, cut:

• 7 (6½"-wide) strips. From strips, cut
8 (6½" × 18½") C rectangles and 16
(6½") B squares.

From blue print #2, cut:

• 6 Stars.

From red print, cut:

• 2 (9½"-wide) strips. Piece strips to
make 1 (9½" × 54½") strip for top of
quilt.

From medium brown print, cut:

• 3 (2½"-wide) strips. Cut strips in half
to make 6 (2½" × 20") strips for strip
sets. (1 is extra.) From extra strip, cut 4
(2½") A squares.

• 7 (2¼"-wide) strips for binding.

Block Assembly

1. Join 1 light print strip and 2 dark
blue print strips as shown in *Strip Set
#1 Diagram*. Make 7 blue Strip Set
#1. From strip sets, cut 42 (2½"-
wide) #1 segments.

Strip Set 1 Diagram

2. In the same manner, join 1 light print
strip and 2 red print strips to make
1 red Strip Set #1. Make 4 red Strip
Set #1. From strip sets, cut 16
(2½"-wide) #1 segments.

3. In the same manner, join 1 brown
print strip and 2 light print strips
as shown in *Strip Set #2 Diagram*.

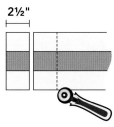

2½"

Strip Set 2 Diagram

Make 4 Strip Set #2. From strip sets, cut 16 (2½"-wide) #2 segments.

4. Referring to *Block A Diagrams,* join 2 matching #1 segments and 1 #2 segment to complete 1 Block A. Make 21 blue Block A and 7 red Block A.

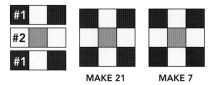

MAKE 21   MAKE 7

Block A Diagrams

5. Lay out 4 matching red print A squares, 4 matching light print A squares, and 1 medium brown print A square. Join squares into rows; join rows to complete 1 Block B *(Block B Diagrams).* Make 4 Block B.

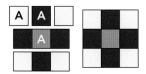

Block B Diagrams

Quilt Assembly

1. Lay out 5 Block A and 4 blue print #1 B squares as shown in *Corner Unit Diagrams.* Join blocks into rows; join rows to make 1 Corner Unit. Make 4 Corner Units.

2. Lay out 2 blue Block A, 1 Block B, and 2 blue print #1 C rectangles. Join to make 1 Side Unit *(Side Unit Diagrams).* Make 4 Side Units.

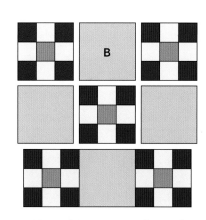

B

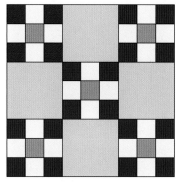

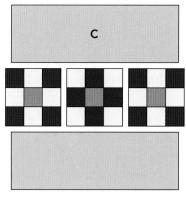

Corner Unit Diagrams

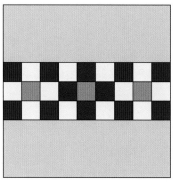

C

Side Unit Diagrams

3. Referring to *Quilt Top Assembly Diagram,* lay out America square, Side Units, and Corner Units. Join into rows; join rows.

4. Referring to photo on page 102, fuse stars and letters to red print strip. Stitch around edges of stars and letters with matching thread and narrow zigzag stitch.

5. Add appliquéd strip to top of quilt.

Finishing

1. Divide backing into 2 (1¾-yard) lengths. Join panels lengthwise. Seam will run horizontally.

2. Layer backing, batting, and quilt top; baste. Quilt as desired. Quilt shown was quilted with diagonal crosshatching *(Quilting Diagram).*

3. Join 2¼"-wide medium brown print strips into 1 continuous piece for straight-grain French-fold binding. Add binding to quilt.

Quilting Diagram

Quilt Top Assembly Diagram

DESIGNER

Jill Reid loves creating new designs using reproduction fabrics. She also enjoys making new versions of antique quilts.

Contact her at: longwood.nj@verizon.net ✻

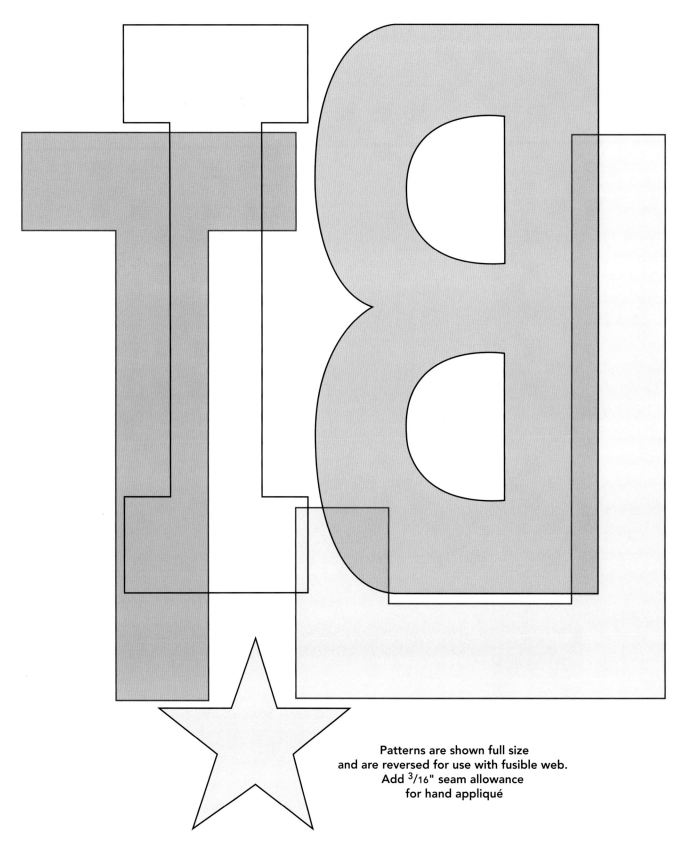

**Patterns are shown full size
and are reversed for use with fusible web.
Add 3/16" seam allowance
for hand appliqué**

Waving Old Glory

Grab a collection of red, white, and blue prints and make this patriotic quilt designed by Toby Lischko.

Size: 69" × 81"

Blocks: 20 (12") Log Cabin blocks

MATERIALS

⅞ yard cream print #1 for blocks

½ yard cream print #2 for pieced border

1½ yards navy print #1 for blocks and outer border

⅞ yard navy print #2 for blocks

⅜ yard navy print #3 for pieced border

⅞ yard blue print #1 for blocks and inner border

⅜ yard blue print #2 for blocks

½ yard red print #1 for blocks

1 yard red print #2 for blocks and borders

1 yard red print #3 for blocks and binding

⅜ yard light red print for blocks

Paper-backed fusible web

5 yards backing fabric

Twin-size quilt batting

Cutting

Measurements include ¼" seam allowances. Border strips are exact length needed. You may want to make them longer to allow for piecing variations. Pattern for Star is on page 111. Follow manufacturer's instructions for using fusible web.

From cream print #1, cut:

• 4 (6½"-wide) strips. From strips, cut 20 (6½") A squares.

From cream print #2, cut:

• 8 (2"-wide) strips for strip sets.

From navy print #1, cut:

• 8 (5"-wide) strips. Piece strips to make 2 (5" × 72½") side outer borders and 2 (5" × 69½") top and bottom outer borders.

• 4 (2"-wide) strips. From strips, cut 20 (2" × 8") C rectangles.

From navy print #2, cut:

• 5 (2"-wide) strips. From strips, cut 20 (2" × 9½") D rectangles.

• 20 Stars.

From navy print #3, cut:

• 4 (2"-wide) strips for strip sets.

From blue print #1, cut:

• 13 (2"-wide) strips. Piece 6 strips to make 2 (2" × 60½") side inner borders and 2 (2" × 51½") top and bottom inner borders. From remaining strips, cut 20 (2" × 11") E rectangles.

From blue print #2, cut:

• 5 (2"-wide) strips. From strips, cut 20 (2" × 9½") D rectangles.

From red print #1, cut:

• 7 (2"-wide) strips. From strips, cut 20 (2" × 11") E rectangles.

From red print #2, cut:

• 15 (2"-wide) strips. Piece 7 strips to make 2 (2" × 69½") side middle borders and 2 (2" × 60½") top and bottom middle borders. From 4 strips, cut 20 (2" × 8") C rectangles. Remaining strips are for strip sets.

From red print #3, cut:

• 9 (2¼"-wide) strips for binding.

• 7 (2"-wide) strips. From strips, cut 20 (2" × 12½") F rectangles.

From light red print, cut:

• 4 (2"-wide) strips. From strips, cut 20 (2" × 6½") B rectangles.

Block Assembly

1. Lay out 1 cream print #1 A square and 1 set of B–F rectangles as shown in *Block Assembly Diagrams*.

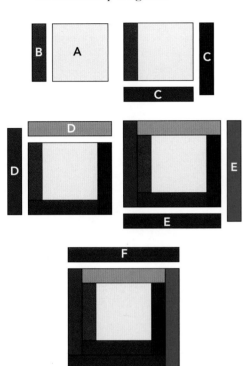

Block Assembly Diagrams

2. Join rectangles to center square, working counter-clockwise in alphabetical order to complete 1 Log Cabin block background *(Block Diagram)*.

Block Diagram

3. Position 1 star atop block; fuse in place.

4. Machine appliqué star to background using matching thread to complete 1 block. Make 20 blocks.

Pieced Border Assembly

1. Join 1 cream print #2 strip and 1 navy print #3 strip as shown in *Strip Set Diagram*. Make 4 navy strip sets. From strip sets, cut 80 (2"-wide) navy segments.

Strip Set Diagram

2. In the same manner, make 4 red strip sets using cream print #2 and red print #2 strips. From strip sets, cut 80 (2"-wide) red segments.

3. Join 1 navy segment and 1 red segment as shown in *Four Patch Unit Diagrams*. Make 80 Four Patch Units.

Four Patch Unit Diagrams

4. Referring to *Quilt Top Assembly Diagram*, join 21 Four Patch Units to make 1 pieced side border. Make 2 pieced side borders.

5. In the same manner, make top pieced border using 19 Four Patch Units. Repeat for bottom pieced border.

Quilt Assembly

1. Lay out blocks as shown in *Quilt Top Assembly Diagram*. Join blocks into rows; join rows to complete quilt center.

2. Add blue print #1 side inner borders to quilt center. Add blue print #1 top and bottom inner borders to quilt.

3. Repeat for pieced borders, red print #2 middle borders, and navy print #1 outer borders.

Finishing

1. Divide backing into 2 (2½-yard) lengths. Cut 1 piece in half lengthwise to make 2 narrow panels. Join 1 narrow panel to each side of wider panel; press seam allowances toward narrow panels.

2. Layer backing, batting, and quilt top; baste. Quilt as desired. Quilt shown was quilted in the ditch, with star rays in blocks, and with crosshatching and wavy lines in borders *(Quilting Diagram)*.

3. Join 2¼"-wide red print #3 strips into 1 continuous piece for straight-grain French-fold binding. Add binding to quilt.

Quilting Diagram

Quilt Top Assembly Diagram

TRIED & TRUE

Give this design a folk art look with fabrics from the Heart and Soul collection by Whimsicals for Red Rooster Fabrics.

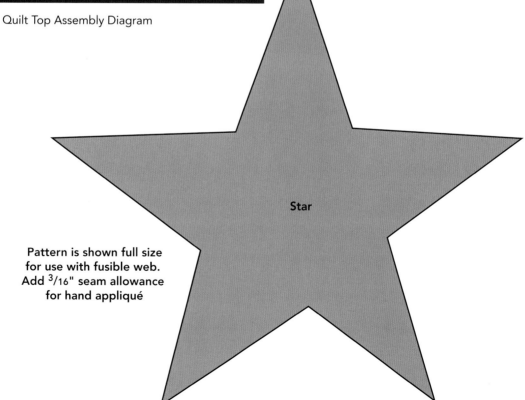

Star

Pattern is shown full size
for use with fusible web.
Add $3/16$" seam allowance
for hand appliqué

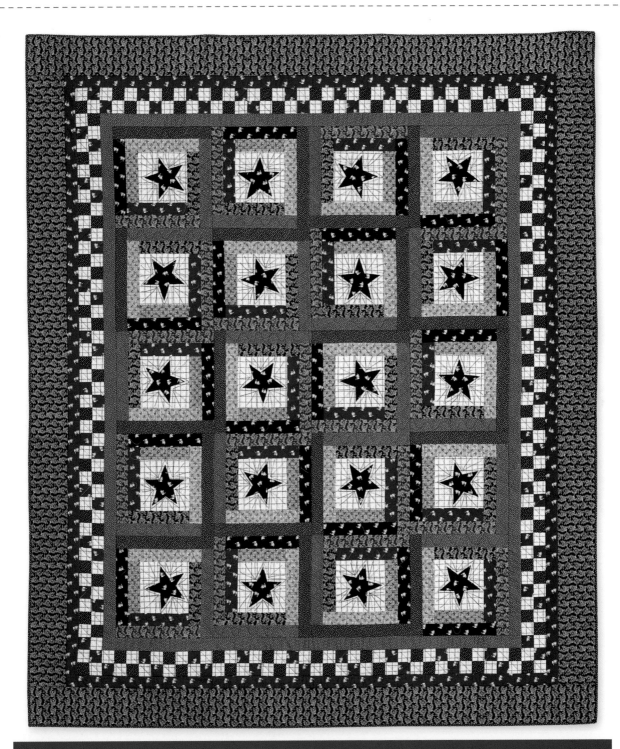

DESIGNER

Toby Lischko is an award-winning quilter who designs quilts, and makes quilts for fabric companies. She is the author of *St. Louis Stars*, published by Kansas City Star Books.

Contact her at:

tlischko@yahoo.com • www.gatewayquiltsnstuff.com ✳

SIZE OPTIONS

	Twin (69" × 93")	Queen (93" × 105")
Blocks	24	42
Setting	4 × 6	6 × 7

MATERIALS

Cream Print #1	⅞ yard	1⅜ yards
Cream Print #2	⅝ yard	1 yard
Navy Print #1	1⅝ yards	2⅛ yards
Navy Print #2	1 yard	1⅝ yards
Navy Print #3	⅜ yard	½ yard
Blue Print #1	1 yard	1⅜ yards
Blue Print #2	½ yard	¾ yard
Red Print #1	½ yard	1 yard
Red Print #2	1⅛ yards	1⅝ yards
Red Print #3	1⅛ yards	1⅝ yards
Light Red Print	⅜ yard	½ yard
Backing Fabric	5½ yards	8½ yards
Batting	Full-size	King-size

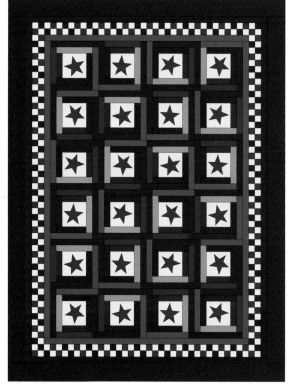

Twin

Queen

America

Patriotic prints featuring the Statue of Liberty seem to sing
America the Beautiful in this bright little quilt.

Size: 36" × 44"

Blocks: 1 (12") Large Star block
3 (8") Medium Star blocks
17 (4") Small Star blocks

MATERIALS

1½ yards beige print

⅜ yard tan print

⅝ yard multicolor print #1

⅝ yard multicolor print #2

1 fat eighth★ blue-and-red print

½ yard blue-and-tan print

½ yard red print

½ yard blue print

1 fat quarter★★ gold print

1½ yards backing fabric

Crib-size quilt batting

★fat eighth = 9" × 20"

★★fat quarter = 18" × 20"

Cutting

Measurements include ¼" seam
allowances. Border strips are exact
length needed. You may want to make
them longer to allow for piecing
variations.

From beige print, cut:
- 1 (8½" × 24½") I rectangle, centering
large Statue of Liberty.
- 2 (4½" × 12½") J rectangles, centering
small Statue of Liberty in each.

From tan print, cut:
- 1 (2⅞"-wide) strip. From strip, cut 8
(2⅞") squares and 4 (2½") F squares.
Cut 2⅞" squares in half diagonally to
make 16 half-square E triangles.
- 2 (1⅞"-wide) strips. From strips, cut
32 (1⅞") squares. Cut squares in half
diagonally to make 64 half-square G
triangles.
- 1 (1½"-wide) strip. From strip,
cut 16 (1½") H squares.

From multicolor print #1, cut:
- 1 (4½"-wide) strip. From strip, cut 2
(4½") D squares and 8 (2⅞") squares.
Cut 2⅞" squares in half diagonally to
make 16 half-square E triangles.
- 5 (2½"-wide) strips. From strips,
cut 2 (2½" × 40½") side borders,
2 (2½" × 36½") top and bottom
borders, and 13 (2½") F squares.
- 1 (1⅞"-wide) strip. From strip, cut
16 (1⅞") squares. Cut squares in half

diagonally to make 32 half-square G
triangles.
- 1 (1½"-wide) strip. From strip,
cut 16 (1½") H squares.

From multicolor print #2, cut:
- 1 (6½"-wide) strip. From strip, cut 1
(6½") A square and 4 (2½") F squares.
- 5 (2¼"-wide) strips for binding.

**From blue-and-red print fat eighth,
cut:**
- 1 (4½"-wide) strip. From strip,
cut 2 (4½") D squares.

From blue-and-tan print, cut:
- 1 (3⅞"-wide) strip. From strip, cut
4 (3⅞") squares. Cut squares in half
diagonally to make 8 half-square B
triangles.
- 1 (3½"-wide) strip. From strip, cut 4
(3½") C squares and 4 (2½") F squares.
- 2 (1⅞"-wide) strips. From strips, cut
36 (1⅞") squares. Cut squares in half
diagonally to make 72 half-square G
triangles.
- 1 (1½"-wide) strip. From strip,
cut 20 (1½") H squares.

From red print, cut:

- 1 (4½"-wide) strip. From strip, cut 6 (4½") D squares.
- 1 (3⅞"-wide) strip. From strip, cut 4 (3⅞") squares. Cut squares in half diagonally to make 8 half-square B triangles.
- 1 (2⅞"-wide) strip. From strip, cut 8 (2⅞") squares. Cut squares in half diagonally to make 16 half-square E triangles.
- 1 (2½"-wide) strip. From strip, cut 8 (2½") F squares.
- 1 (1⅞"-wide) strip. From strip, cut 20 (1⅞") squares. Cut squares in half diagonally to make 40 half-square G triangles.

From blue print, cut:

- 1 (4½"-wide) strip. From strip, cut 7 (4½") D squares.
- 1 (2⅞"-wide) strip. From strip, cut 8 (2⅞") squares. Cut squares in half diagonally to make 16 half-square E triangles.
- 2 (1⅞"-wide) strips. From strips, cut 32 (1⅞") squares. Cut squares in half diagonally to make 64 half-square G triangles.
- 1 (1½"-wide) strip. From strip, cut 16 (1½") H squares.

From gold print fat quarter, cut:

- 2 (4½"-wide) strips. From strips, cut 7 (4½") D squares.

Block Assembly

1. Join 1 red print B triangle and 1 blue-and-tan print B triangle as shown in *Triangle-Square Diagrams*. Make 8 large triangle-squares.

Triangle-Square Diagrams

2. Lay out multicolor print #2 A square, 8 large triangle-squares, and 4 blue-and-tan print C squares as shown in *Large Star Block Assembly Diagram*. Join into rows; join rows to complete large Star block *(Large Star Block Diagram)*.

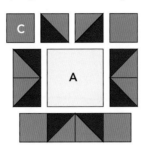

Large Star Block Assembly Diagram

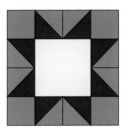

Large Star Block Diagram

3. Make 16 medium triangle-squares using red print E triangles and tan print E triangles.

4. Lay out 1 multicolor print #1 D square, 8 medium triangle-squares, and 4 red print F squares as shown in *Medium Star Block Assembly Diagram*. Join into rows; join rows to complete 1 block *(Medium Star Block Diagrams)*. Make 2 medium Star blocks.

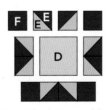

Medium Star Block Assembly Diagram

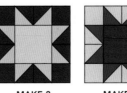

MAKE 2   MAKE 2
Medium Star Block Diagrams

5. In the same manner, make 2 medium Star blocks using 8 blue print E triangles, 8 multicolor print #1 E triangles, 4 multicolor print #1 F squares, and 1 blue-and-red print D square in each.

6. Choose 1 F square, 8 matching G triangles for star points, and 8 matching triangles and 4 H squares for background. Make 1 small Star block as described in Steps #1–#2 *(Small Star Block Diagram)*. Make 17 small Star blocks.

Small Star Block Diagram

Quilt Assembly

1. Lay out Star blocks, I and J rectangles, and red, blue, and gold print D squares as shown in *Quilt Top Assembly Diagram*. Join into sections; join sections to complete quilt center.

2. Add multicolor print #1 side borders to quilt center. Add top and bottom borders to quilt.

Finishing

1. Layer backing, batting, and quilt top; baste. Quilt as desired. Quilt shown was quilted with an allover swirl design *(Quilting Diagram)*.

2. Join 2¼"-wide multicolor print #2 strips into 1 continuous piece for straight-grain French-fold binding. Add binding to quilt.

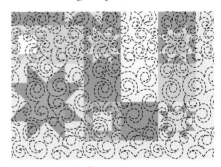

Quilting Diagram

Quilt Top Assembly Diagram

DESIGNER

September Olson is a crafty mother, wife, and graphic designer who lives with her family in Seattle, Washington.
Contact her at: SepDep@hotmail.com ✳

July Jubilee

Celebrate America's birthday with this festive and colorful quilt.
Hang it in a prominent place or use it as a table topper, and let the festivities begin.

Size: 40" × 40"
Blocks: 4 (18") blocks

MATERIALS

1 fat quarter★ red print #1

1 yard red print #2

2 fat quarters★ cream prints

1 fat quarter★ red, white, and blue
  stripe

½ yard blue print

Template material

2¾ yards backing fabric

Crib-size quilt batting

★ fat quarter = 18" × 20"

Cutting

Measurements include ¼" seam allowances. Patterns for E and F are on page 122.

From red print #1 fat quarter, cut:

• 2 (4⅛"-wide) strips. From strips, cut 8 (4⅛") squares. Cut squares in half diagonally to make 16 half-square A triangles.

From red print #2, cut:

• 5 (2¾"-wide) strips. Piece strips to make 4 (2¾" × 44") border strips.

• 5 (2¼"-wide) strips for binding.

• 28 E.

• 4 F.

From cream print #1 fat quarter, cut:

• 2 (4⅛"-wide) strips. From strips, cut 8 (4⅛") squares. Cut squares in half diagonally to make 16 half-square A triangles.

From cream print #2 fat quarter, cut:

• 3 (5⅜"-wide) strips. From strips, cut 8 (5⅜") squares. Cut squares in half diagonally to make 16 half-square B triangles.

From red, white, and blue stripe fat quarter, cut:

• 3 (5⅜"-wide) strips. From strips, cut 8 (5⅜") squares. Referring to *Cutting Diagrams*, cut 4 squares in half diagonally from upper left to lower right and cut 4 in half diagonally from lower left to upper right to make 16 half-square B triangles.

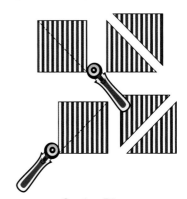

Cutting Diagrams

From blue print, cut:

• 2 (7¼"-wide) strips. From strips, cut 8 (7¼") squares and 2 (4⅛") squares. Cut 7¼" squares in half diagonally to make 16 half-square C triangles. Cut 4⅛" squares in half diagonally to make 4 half-square A triangles.

Block Assembly

1. Join 1 red print #1 A triangle and 1 cream print #1 A triangle as shown in *Triangle-Square Diagrams.* Make 16 triangle-squares.

Triangle-Square Diagrams

2. Join 4 triangle-squares to make 1 Pinwheel Unit *(Pinwheel Unit Diagrams).* Make 4 Pinwheel Units.

Pinwheel Unit Diagrams

3. Add 2 red print #2 E to 1 cream print #2 B triangle, mitering corners as shown in *Corner Unit Diagrams.* Make 12 Corner Units.

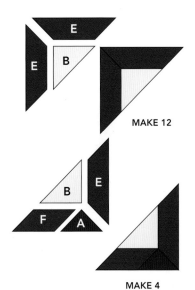

MAKE 12

MAKE 4

Corner Unit Diagrams

4. In a similar manner, make 4 Corner Units using 1 cream print #2 B triangle, 1 red print #2 E, 1 red print #2 F, and 1 blue print A triangle in each.

5. Lay out 1 Pinwheel Unit, 4 stripe B triangles, and 4 blue print C triangles as shown in *Block Center Diagrams.* Join to complete 1 Block Center.

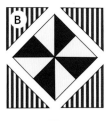

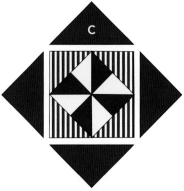

Block Center Diagrams

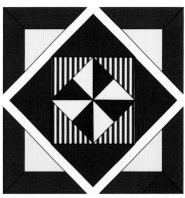

Block Assembly Diagram

Block Diagram

6. Lay out Block Center and 4 Corner Units as shown in *Block Assembly Diagram.* Join to complete 1 block *(Block Diagram).* Make 4 blocks. **NOTE:** Refer to *Quilt Top Assembly Diagram* on page 121 when assembling the blocks. Correct placement of Corner Units with the blue print A triangles will create a pinwheel in the center of quilt.

Quilt Assembly

1. Lay out blocks as shown in *Quilt Top Assembly Diagram.*

2. Join blocks into rows; join rows to complete quilt center.

3. Add borders to quilt center, mitering corners.

Sew **Smart**™

For instructions on mitering borders, see *Sew Easy: Mitered Borders* on page 123.

Finishing

1. Divide backing into 2 (1⅞-yard) lengths. Cut 1 piece in half lengthwise to make 2 narrow panels. Join 1 narrow panel to wider panel. Remaining panel is extra and can be used to make a hanging sleeve.

2. Layer backing, batting, and quilt top; baste. Quilt as desired. Quilt shown was quilted with freehand stars *(Quilting Diagram).*

3. Join 2¼"-wide red print #2 strips into 1 continuous piece for straight-grain French-fold binding. Add binding to quilt.

Quilt Top Assembly Diagram

Quilting Diagram

TRIED & TRUE

We made our block using prints and linen-look solids from the Sausalito collection by P&B Textiles.

DESIGNER

Terry Griffin started quilting and sewing with the 4-H Club in her small community when she was eight years old. She has continued using that knowledge throughout her life. Terry thanks all those "aunties" who taught her when her Thankfully Sew Pattern Company was born.

Contact her at:
www.thankfullysew.com ✳

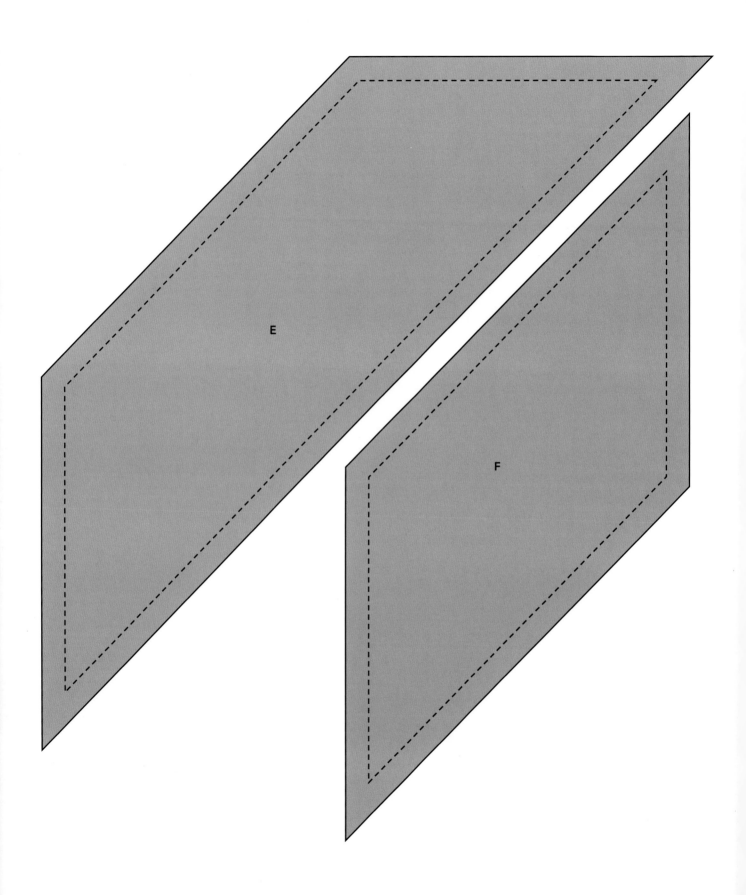

E

F

Mitered Borders

The subtle seam of a mitered corner creates the illusion of a continuous line around the quilt. Mitered corners are ideal for striped fabric borders or multiple plain borders.

1. Referring to *Measuring Diagram*, measure your quilt length through the middle of the quilt rather than along the edges. In the same manner, measure quilt width. Add to your measurements twice the planned width of the border plus 2". Trim borders to these measurements.

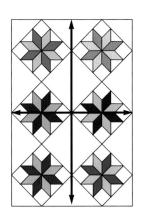

Measuring Diagram

2. On wrong side of quilt top, mark ¼" seam allowances at each corner.

3. Fold quilt top in half and place a pin at the center of the quilt side. Fold border in half and mark center with pin.

4. With right sides facing and raw edges aligned, match center pins on the border and the quilt. Working from the center out, pin the border to the quilt, right sides facing. The border will extend beyond the quilt edges. Do not trim the border.

5. Sew the border to the quilt. Start and stop stitching ¼" from the corner of the quilt top, backstitching at each end. Press the seam allowance toward the border. Add the remaining borders in the same manner.

6. With right sides facing, fold the quilt diagonally as shown in *Mitering Diagram 1*, aligning the raw edges of the adjacent borders. Pin securely.

7. Align a ruler along the diagonal fold, as shown in *Mitering Diagram 2*. Holding the ruler firmly, mark a line from the end of the border seam to the raw edge.

8. Start machine stitching at the beginning of the marked line, backstitch, and then stitch on the line out to the raw edge.

9. Unfold the quilt to be sure that the corner lies flat *(Mitered Borders Diagram)*. Correct the stitching if necessary. Trim the seam allowance to ¼".

10. Miter the remaining corners. Press the corner seams open.

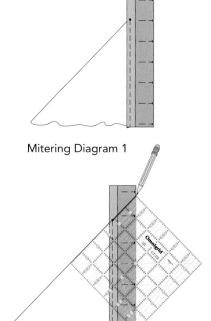

Mitering Diagram 1

Mitering Diagram 2

Mitered Borders Diagram

QUILT BY **Liz Porter and Marianne Fons.**
MACHINE QUILTED BY **Jean Nolte.**

Stars & Stripes Sampler

Size: (80" × 98")

We used a wide variety of red, blue, gold, and cream print, stripe, and plaid fabrics, with a few greens and browns added, for our sampler. Materials for each block are listed with each set of instructions. If you are pulling fabrics from your stash or wish to purchase the fabrics for this quilt, an estimate of what you'll need is below.

MATERIALS

10–20 fat quarters★★ assorted cream/tan prints

30–40 fat eighths★ or fat quarters★★ red, blue, gold, brown, and green prints

¼ yard each of 10–15 assorted prints for Life, Liberty, Pursuit of Happiness, and Liberty Star blocks

¾ yard each of tan plaid for eagle background and cream print for Continental Rose background

½ yard each navy print for eagle, navy plaid for Pursuit of Happiness, and tan print for Freedom Star Section

½ yard red-and-white stripe for inner border

1⅝ yards navy print for outer border

¾ yard red print for binding

7½ yards backing fabric

Queen-size quilt batting

★fat eighth = 9" × 20"

★★fat quarter = 18" × 20"

Old Glory Flag Blocks

Finished size:

1 (10" × 20") vertical Flag block

2 (18" × 10") horizontal Flag blocks

MATERIALS

(for 1 flag)

Scrap (at least 9" square) navy blue print

Scraps (at least 6" square) of 1 or 2 gold prints

¼ yard red print

⅛ yard tan print

Cutting (for 1 vertical flag)

From navy blue print, cut:

- 4 (2½") squares.
- 2 (2⅞") squares. Cut squares in half diagonally to make 4 half-square triangles.

From gold print(s), cut:

- 1 (2½") center square.
- 2 (2⅞") squares. Cut squares in half diagonally to make 4 half-square triangles.

From red print, cut:

- 2 (2½"-wide) strips. From strips, cut 1 (2½" × 20½") A strip and 2 (2½" × 14½") B strips.

From tan print, cut:

- 1 (2½"-wide) strip. From strip, cut 1 (2½" × 20½") A strip and 1 (2½" × 14½") B strip.

Cutting (for 1 horizontal flag)

From navy blue print, cut:

- 4 (2½") squares.
- 2 (2⅞") squares. Cut squares in half

diagonally to make 4 half-square triangles.

From gold print(s), cut:

- 1 (2½") center square.
- 2 (2⅞") squares. Cut squares in half diagonally to make 4 half-square triangles.

From red print, cut:

- 2 (2½"-wide) strips. From strips, cut 1 (2½" × 18½") C strip and 2 (2½" × 12½") D strips.

From tan print, cut:

- 1 (2½"-wide) strips. From strips, cut 1 (2½" × 18½") C strip and 1 (2½" × 12½") D strip.

Star Assembly

1. Join 1 navy print triangle and gold print triangle as shown in *Triangle-Square Diagrams*. Make 4 triangle-squares.

Triangle-Square Diagrams

2. Lay out triangle-squares, navy print squares, and gold print square as shown in *Star Block Assembly Diagram*. Join into rows; join rows to complete Star block *(Star Block Diagram)*.

Star Block Assembly Diagram

Star Block Diagram

3. Make 1 Star block for each flag.

Vertical Flag Assembly

1. Lay out Star block and red and tan print A and B strips as shown in *Vertical Flag Assembly Diagram*.

2. Join to complete vertical flag *(Vertical Flag Diagram)*.

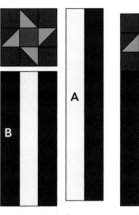

Vertical Flag
Assembly Diagram

Vertical Flag
Diagram

Horizontal Flag Assembly

1. Lay out Star block and red and tan print C and D strips as shown in *Horizontal Flag Assembly Diagram*.

2. Join to complete horizontal flag *(Horizontal Flag Diagram)*. Make 2 Horizontal Flag blocks.

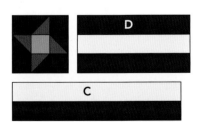
Horizontal Flag Assembly Diagram

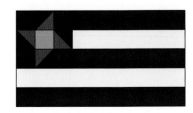
Horizontal Flag Diagram

Little Long Flag

Finished size: 1 (18" × 6") block

MATERIALS

1 (3½" × 6½") rectangle navy print
Fat eighth★ red print
Fat eighth★ tan print
★fat eighth = 9" × 20"

Cutting

From red print, cut:

• 3 (1½"-wide) strips. From strips, cut 2 (1½" × 18½") strips and 1 (1½" × 12½") strip.

From tan print, cut:

• 3 (1½"-wide) strips. From strips, cut 1 (1½" × 18½") strip and 2 (1½" × 12½") strips.

Flag Assembly

1. Lay out navy print rectangle and red and tan print strips as shown in *Little Long Flag Assembly Diagram.*

Little Long Flag Assembly Diagram

2. Join to complete Little Long Flag (*Little Long Flag Diagram*).

Little Long Flag Diagram

Facts About our Flag

• No one knows for sure, but Congressman Francis Hopkinson probably designed the first American flag, and some historians believe that Betsy Ross, a Philadelphia seamstress, may have made it.

• On June 14, 1777, the Continental Congress passed the first Flag Act: "Resolved, that the flag of the United States be made of thirteen stripes, alternate red and white; that the union be thirteen stars, white in a blue field, representing a new Constellation."

• According to the U.S. Code, the flag, whether displayed horizontally or vertically, should be arranged so that the "union" (the field of stars) is uppermost and to the observer's left.

• When a new State is admitted, one star is added to the field of stars. That addition is to take effect on the next July 4th after the admission of the State. This practice was established in 1818, and signed into law by President James Monroe.

• In 1885, a Wisconsin schoolteacher arranged for students to observe June 14 (the 108th anniversary of the official adoption of the Stars and Stripes) as Flag Birthday. Although our flag's birthday was honored after that in many local and state celebrations, it was not until August 3, 1949, that President Harry Truman signed an official Act of Congress designating June 14 of each year as National Flag Day.

• The nickname "Old Glory" was given to our flag in 1831, by Massachusetts shipmaster Captain Stephen Driver when he was given a beautiful flag of 24 stars. As the banner opened to the ocean breeze for the first time, he exclaimed, "Old Glory!" Retiring to Nashville, Captain Driver preserved this flag during the Civil War by stitching it into a quilt. When Union Soldiers captured Nashville in 1862, he opened the quilt so that "Old Glory," instead of a much smaller banner, could fly over the capital of Tennessee. Although he was then sixty years old, Driver climbed the tower himself to install his beloved flag.

Schoolhouse Blocks

Finished size: 3 (12") blocks

MATERIALS

(for 1 block)

1 (1½" × 10") strip each of 2 gold
  prints for window strip set
1 (2" × 4½") rectangle brown print
  for door
Fat eighth★ red print for house
  front and house peak
Fat eighth★ red print for house side
Scrap (at least 5" × 11½") for roof
Scrap (at least 6" × 13") for sky
  (background)
Scrap (at least 3" × 6") for chimneys
5" × 13" piece of paper for
  foundation
★fat eighth = 9" × 20"

Cutting

**From house front and peak fabric,
cut:**
• 1 (5½") square for foundation piecing
  house peak (F).
• 2 (1¾" × 4½") A rectangles.
• 1 (2½" × 4½") B rectangle.

From house side fabric, cut:
• 2 (1½" × 2½") C rectangles.
• 2 (2½" × 8½") D rectangles.

From sky fabric, cut:
• 2 (3½" × 5½") rectangles for foundation piecing (G).
• 2 (2½") J squares.
• 1 (2½" × 5½") H rectangle.

From chimney fabric, cut:
• 2 (2" × 2½") I rectangles.

Roof Section Assembly

1. Draw a 4" × 12" rectangle on a 5" ×
   13" piece of tracing paper or other
   lightweight paper.
2. Referring to *Roof Section Foundation
   Pattern Diagram*, measure and draw
   lines as shown. (Pattern is reversed
   because fabrics will be placed on
   opposite side of paper.) Draw a ¼"
   seam allowance around all four sides.

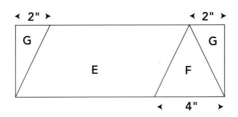

Roof Section Foundation Pattern Diagram

3. Referring to *Sew Easy: Paper
   Foundation Piecing* on page 27, piece
   roof section in alphabetical order.
4. Trim roof section on outer drawn
   lines of paper pattern.
5. Join H rectangle, I rectangles, and
   J squares to make chimney section
   as shown in *Block Assembly Diagram*.
   Make 3 Schoolhouse blocks.

House Section Assembly

1. Referring to *Block Assembly Diagram*,
   join 1 A rectangle to each side of
   door rectangle. Add B rectangle to
   top edge to make house front.

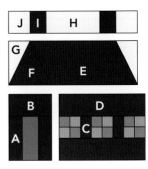

Block Assembly Diagram

2. Join window strips to make strip set.
   From strip set, cut 6 (1½"-wide) segments. Join 2 segments to make 1
   Four Patch Unit.
3. Lay out Four Patch Units and C and
   D rectangles as shown. Join Four
   Patch Units and C rectangles to form
   window section. Add D rectangles to
   top and bottom to make house side
   as shown. Join house front to house
   side.
4. Join chimney, roof, and house
   sections to complete block *(Block
   Diagram)*.
5. Make 3 Schoolhouse blocks.

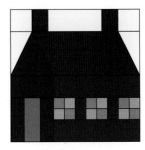

Block Diagram

Declaration Star Blocks

Finished size: 7 (10") blocks

Declaration Star Section Diagram

MATERIALS

(for 1 block)

2 (5½") squares print #1 for Four Patch Unit

2 (5½") squares print #2 for Four Patch Unit

1 (8") square print #3 for circle

1 (7") square print #4 for star

Paper-backed fusible web **NOTE:** To reduce bulk in fusible appliqué, refer to *Sew Easy: Windowing Fusible Appliqué* on page 13.

Four Patch Assembly

1. Lay out print #1 and #2 squares as shown in *Four Patch Unit Diagrams.*

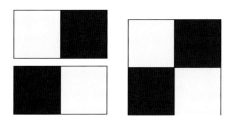

Four Patch Unit Diagrams

2. Join into rows; join rows to complete Four Patch Unit.

Block Assembly

1. Position circle atop Four Patch Unit; fuse in place. Machine or hand blanket stitch around circle (*Blanket Stitch Diagram*).

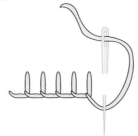

Blanket Stitch Diagram

2. If desired, trim background fabric from behind circle, cutting a scant ¼" inside stitching.

3. Position star atop circle; fuse in place. Machine or hand blanket stitch around star. If desired, trim background fabric from behind star. Make 7 Declaration Star blocks.

Declaration Star Section Assembly

1. Arrange 6 blocks as shown in *Declaration Star Section Diagram*. Join into rows; join rows.

On July 2, 1776, in Philadelphia, Richard Henry Lee and John Adams introduced a resolution declaring independence from Great Britain and explaining the Colonists' grievances against King George III. The Declaration was officially adopted by the Continental Congress on July 4, 1776.

**Patterns are shown full size
for use with fusible web. Add $^3/_{16}$"
seam allowance for hand appliqué**

American Eagle

Finished size: 1 (26" × 20") block

MATERIALS

1 (26½" × 20½") rectangle tan
plaid for background

½ yard navy print for eagle

Scrap (at least 4" × 5½") navy/
cream stripe for shield

Scraps (at least 9" × 9") red, green,
and gold prints for band on
shield, stars, arrows, leaves, and
penny circles

Paper-backed fusible web

Green embroidery floss

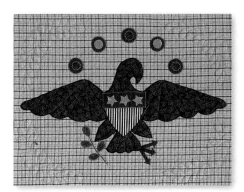

Cutting & Assembly

1. Using patterns on pages 132–133,
trace Eagle, Shield, Shield Band, 3
Stars, Arrows, 4 Leaves, and 5 Small
and 5 Large Penny Circles onto
smooth side of fusible web. See *Sew
Easy: Windowing Fusible Appliqué* on
page 13. Fuse shapes to wrong side
of fabric. Cut out appliqué pieces on
drawn lines.

2. Referring to photo and *Master
Pattern Diagram* on page 132, posi-
tion appliqué pieces on background.
Tuck arrow cluster under tip of tail.
Bottom of tail is 3¼" from bottom
edge of background rectangle. Wing
tips are ¾" from sides of rectangle.
Top of head is 5¼" from top edge.
Fuse shapes to background.

3. Stitch shapes to background rectangle using blanket stitch *(Blanket Stitch
Diagram on page 133)*. Embroider
stem using green embroidery floss
and outline stitch *(Outline Stitch
Diagram on page 133)*.

With the completion of the Eagle
block, you can construct Section 1 of
your Sampler. See p. 150.

Continental Rose

Finished size: 1 (18") block

MATERIALS

1 (18½") square cream print for
background

1 fat eighth★ navy print for stars

1 fat eighth★ green print for stems
and leaves

Scrap (at least 6½" × 6½") red
print for outer buds

Scrap (at least 5" × 5") gold print
for inner buds

Paper-backed fusible web

★fat eighth = 9" × 20"

Cutting & Assembly

1. Using patterns on page 134, trace
5 Stars, 4 Outer Buds, 4 Inner Buds,
4 Stems, and 12 Leaves onto smooth
side of fusible web. Roughly cut out
shapes, cutting ¼" outside drawn
lines. See *Sew Easy: Windowing Fusible
Appliqué* on page 13 to window all
shapes except stems. Fuse shapes to
wrong side of fabric. Cut out appliqué pieces on drawn lines.

2. Fold background square in half vertically, horizontally, and diagonally
both ways; lightly press to form
placement guidelines. Referring to
Continental Rose Placement Diagram on
page 134, position appliqué pieces,
working from background to foreground, tucking vine ends under
buds and stars. Fuse pieces in place.

3. Machine blanket or satin stitch using
matching thread.

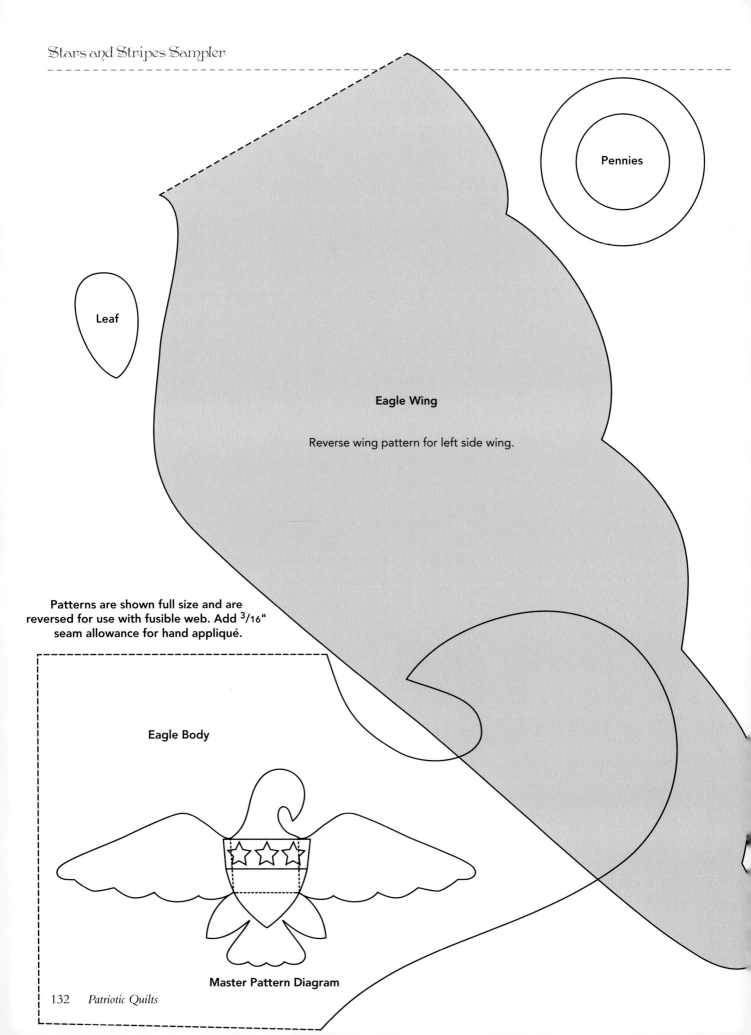

Pennies

Leaf

Eagle Wing

Reverse wing pattern for left side wing.

Patterns are shown full size and are
reversed for use with fusible web. Add 3/16"
seam allowance for hand appliqué.

Eagle Body

Master Pattern Diagram

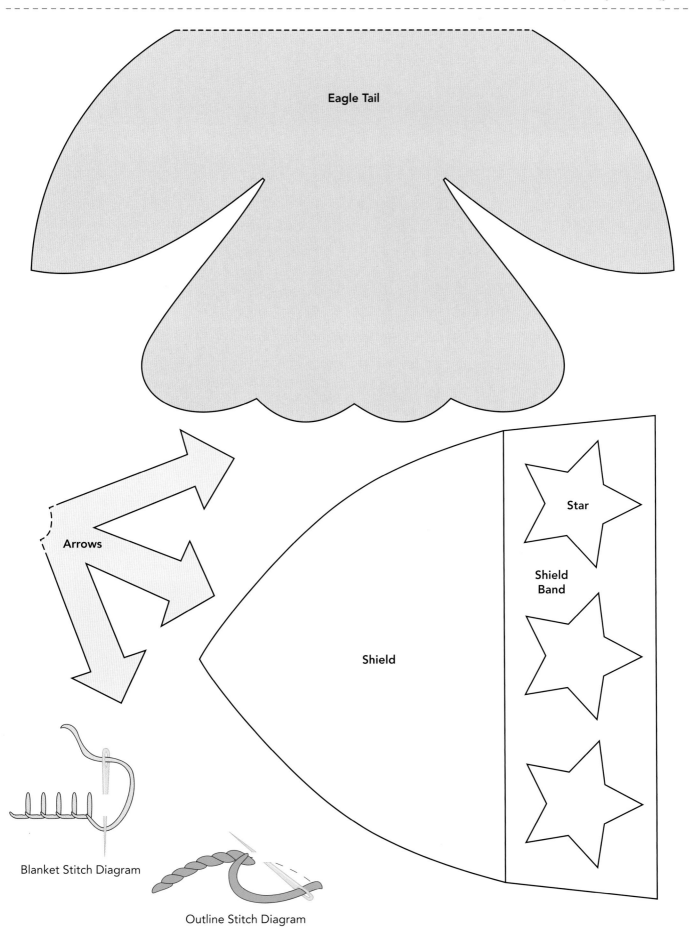

Eagle Tail

Arrows

Shield

Star

Shield
Band

Blanket Stitch Diagram

Outline Stitch Diagram

Patterns are shown full size and are
reversed for use with fusible web. Add $3/16$"
seam allowance for hand appliqué

Continental Rose Placement Diagram

"The flower commonly
known as the rose is
designated and adopted as
the national floral emblem
of the United States of
America . . ."

(FROM THE U.S. CODE)

Boston Star

Finished size: 1 (12") block

MATERIALS

1 fat quarter★ tan print
Scrap (at least 6" × 11") each of
 gold print and navy print
fat quarter★ = 18" × 20"

Cutting

From tan print, cut:

- 1 (4½"-wide) strip. From strip, cut 4 (4½") C squares.

- 1 (5¼") square. Cut square in half diagonally in both directions to make 4 quarter-square A triangles.

From gold print, cut:

- 1 (5¼") square. Cut square in half diagonally in both directions to make 4 quarter-square A triangles.

- 1 (4½") C square.

From navy print, cut:

- 2 (4⅞") squares. Cut squares in half diagonally to make 4 half-square B triangles.

Assembly

1. Join 1 gold print A triangle, 1 tan print A triangle, and 1 navy print B triangle as shown in *Star Point Unit Diagrams*. Make 4 Star Point Units.

2. Lay out Star Point Units, gold print C square, and tan print C squares as shown in *Block Assembly Diagram*.

Star Point Unit Diagrams

Join into rows; join rows to complete block *(Block Diagram)*.

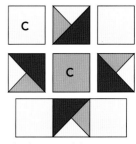

Block Assembly Diagram

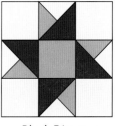

Block Diagram

Lexington Star

Finished size: 1 (12") block

MATERIALS

¼ yard tan print
Scrap (at least 6" × 11") each of
 red print and blue print
1 (2½" × 21") strip gold print

Cutting

From tan print, cut:

- 1 (2½" × 21") strip for strip set.

- 1 (5¼") square. Cut square in half diagonally in both directions to make 4 quarter-square A triangles.

From red print, cut:

- 1 (5¼") square. Cut square in half diagonally in both directions to make 4 quarter-square A triangles.

- 1 (4½") C square.

From blue print, cut:

- 2 (4⅞") squares. Cut squares in half diagonally to make 4 half-square B triangles.

Assembly

1. Join 1 red print A triangle, 1 tan print A triangle, and blue print B triangle as shown in *Star Point Unit Diagrams*. Make 4 Star Point Units.

Star Point Unit Diagrams

---

2. Join 1 tan print strip and 1 gold print strip as shown in *Strip Set Diagram*. From strip set, cut 8 (2½"-wide) segments.

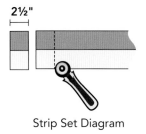

Strip Set Diagram

3. Join 2 segments as shown in *Four Patch Unit Diagrams*. Make 4 Four Patch Units.

Four Patch Unit Diagrams

4. Lay out Star Point Units, Four Patch Units, and red print C square as shown in *Block Assembly Diagram*. Join into rows; join rows to complete block (*Block Diagram*).

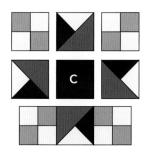

Block Assembly Diagram

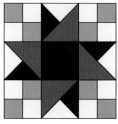

Block Diagram

Concord Star

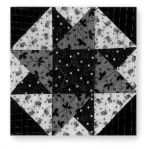

Finished size: 1 (12") block

MATERIALS

Scrap (at least 6" × 11") of red print
Fat eighth★ tan print
Scrap (at least 5" × 11") each of gold print and navy print
★fat eighth = 9" × 20"

Cutting

From red print, cut:

• 1 (5¼") square. Cut square in half diagonally in both directions to make 4 quarter-square A triangles.

• 1 (4½") C square.

From tan print, cut:

• 1 (5¼") square. Cut square in half diagonally in both directions to make 4 quarter-square A triangles.

• 2 (4⅞") squares. Cut squares in half diagonally to make 4 half-square B triangles.

From gold print, cut:

• 2 (4⅞") squares. Cut squares in half diagonally to make 4 half-square B triangles.

From navy print, cut:

• 2 (4⅞") squares. Cut squares in half diagonally to make 4 half-square B triangles.

Assembly

1. Join 1 red print A triangle, 1 tan print A triangle, and 1 gold print B triangle as shown in *Star Point Unit Diagrams*. Make 4 Star Point Units.

Star Point Unit Diagrams

2. Join 1 tan print B triangle and 1 navy print B triangle as shown in *Triangle-Square Diagrams*. Make 4 triangle-squares.

Triangle-Square Diagrams

3. Lay out Star Point Units, triangle-squares, and red print C square as shown in *Block Assembly Diagram*. Join into rows; join rows to complete block (*Block Diagram*).

Block Assembly Diagram

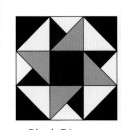

Block Diagram

Bunker Hill Star

Finished size: 1 (12") block

MATERIALS

1 fat eighth★ tan print
Scrap (at least 6" × 11") each of
    red, navy, and gold prints
★fat eighth = 9" × 20"

Cutting

From tan print, cut:

- 1 (5¼") square. Cut square in half diagonally in both directions to make 4 quarter-square A triangles.
- 2 (4⅞") squares. Cut squares in half diagonally to make 4 half-square B triangles.
- 4 (2½") D squares.

From red print, cut:

- 2 (4⅞") squares. Cut squares in half diagonally to make 4 half-square B triangles.

From navy print, cut:

- 2 (4⅞") squares. Cut squares in half diagonally to make 4 half-square B triangles.

From gold print, cut:

- 1 (5¼") square. Cut square in half diagonally in both directions to make 4 quarter-square A triangles.
- 1 (4½") C square.

Assembly

1. Join 1 tan print A triangle, 1 gold print A triangle, and 1 red print B triangle as shown in *Star Point Unit Diagrams*. Make 4 Star Point Units.

Star Point Unit Diagrams

2. Referring to *Diagonal Seams Diagrams*, place 1 tan print D square atop 1 navy print B triangle, right sides facing. Stitch diagonally from corner to corner. Trim ¼" beyond stitching. Press open to reveal triangle.

Diagonal Seams Diagrams

3. Join 1 tan B triangle to diagonal seams unit as shown in *Corner Unit Diagrams*. Make 4 corner units.

Corner Unit Diagrams

4. Lay out Star Point Units, Corner Units, and gold print C square as shown in *Block Assembly Diagram*. Join into rows; join rows to complete block (*Block Diagram*).

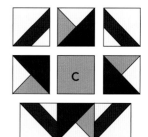

Block Assembly Diagram

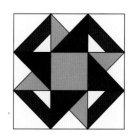

Block Diagram

Struggles between the British and Colonials in the Massachusetts communities of Boston, Lexington, Concord, and Bunker Hill in 1775 were early events that escalated the conflict between England and the New World and resulted in the American Revolution.

Liz's Lucky Stars Blocks

You'll make two blocks at once with Liz's nifty slice-and-sew method!

Finished size: 2 (12") blocks

MATERIALS

1 (13½") square each blue print and red plaid fabric

4 (1" × 40") strips cream plaid to outline stars

12½" square ruler (optional)

Assembly

Note: Make all cuts at least 1½" from corners of squares.

1. Stack both squares with right sides facing up. Using rotary cutter and ruler, cut approximately as shown in *Step 1 Cutting Diagram*. Lay out pieces as shown in *Step 1 Assembly Diagrams* to make 2 units. Each unit will have 1 piece of each fabric. Referring to Step *1 Assembly Diagrams*, stitch cream strip to angled side of 1R piece. Press seam toward cream strip. Trim ends of strip even with edge of square unit. Stitch 2B piece to opposite side of cream strip. In a similar manner, join 1B and 2R pieces with cream strip between

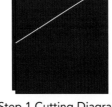

Step 1 Cutting Diagram

 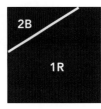

Step 1 Assembly Diagrams

pieces. You will have 2 pieced squares, each with both fabrics separated by a cream strip.

2. Stack pieced squares from Step 1, aligning cream strips so all pieces are in the same position. Make a cut similar to that shown in *Step 2 Cutting Diagram*. One end of cut should go through center of end of light strip. Lay out pieces as shown in *Step 2 Assembly Diagrams*. Join cream

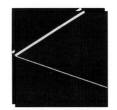

Step 2 Cutting Diagram

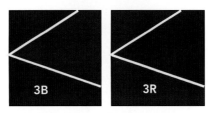

Step 2 Assembly Diagrams

strip to angled side of 3B piece. Join upper unit to opposite side of cream strip. In a similar manner, join 3R piece to upper unit with cream strip between.

3. Stack pieced squares from Step 2, keeping them aligned. Cut as shown in *Step 3 Cutting Diagram*, cutting through center of end of light strip. Lay out pieces as shown in *Step 3 Assembly Diagrams*. Join sections with cream strip between sections to make 2 pieced squares. **Note:** Things may look a bit confusing at this stage so pay careful attention to the assembly diagrams.

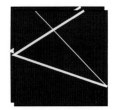

Step 3 Cutting Diagram

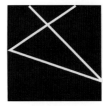 

Step 3 Assembly Diagrams

4. Stack pieced squares from Step 3, keeping them aligned. Make a cut similar to that shown in *Step 4 Cutting Diagram,* cutting through center of end of light strip. Lay out pieces as shown in *Step 4 Assembly Diagrams.* Join sections with cream strip between sections to make 2 pieced squares. **Note:** You will begin to see each star form!

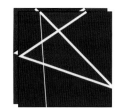

Step 4 Cutting Diagram

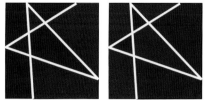

Step 4 Assembly Diagrams

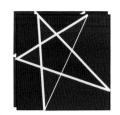

Step 5 Cutting Diagram

Step 5 Assembly Diagrams

Block Diagrams

With the completion of the Lucky Stars blocks, you can construct Section 2 of your Sampler. See p. 150.

5. Stack pieced squares from Step 4, keeping them aligned. Make a cut similar to that shown in *Step 5 Cutting Diagram*. Lay out pieces as

shown in *Step 5 Assembly Diagrams*. Join sections with cream strip between sections to complete 2 Lucky Star blocks *(Block Diagrams)*.

6. Trim blocks to 12½" square.

July 4th Star Blocks

Finished size: 4 (6") blocks

MATERIALS

(for 1 block)

4 (3½") squares light print for background

2 (2" × 3½") rectangles each red and blue prints for star points

Assembly

1. Fold light print square in half and pinch to form center guide on one edge of square.

2. Place 1 rectangle atop 1 background square as shown in *Diagonal Seams Diagrams*. Stitch from corner to corner as shown.

Diagonal Seams Diagrams

Tip: When placing rectangle atop background square, let tip of rectangle extend slightly over top edge of bottom square.

3. Fold back rectangle and finger press to check that corners align.

4. Trim away excess background square and top rectangle ¼" beyond stitching. Press to complete 1 quadrant. Make 2 red and 2 blue quadrants.

5. Lay out 4 quadrants as shown in *Block Assembly Diagram*. Join quadrants into rows; join rows to complete block *(Block Diagram)*. Make 4 blocks.

Block Assembly Diagram

Block Diagram

With the completion of the July 4th Star blocks, you can construct Section 3 of your Sampler. See p. 150.

Life Blocks

Finished size: 3 (10") blocks

MATERIALS
(for 3 blocks)

2 (6") squares each red print, navy print, and blue plaid

40"-long strips of assorted gold, red, blue, and cream fabrics in various widths ranging from 1"–2½" wide.

Assembly

1. Placing wider strips on top and bottom, join assorted strips to make a strip set that measures 6"–6½" from top to bottom as shown in *Strip Set Diagram*. Press seam allowances in one direction.

Strip Set Diagram

2. Draw a cutting line diagonally from corner to corner on wrong side of 1 square. Draw sewing lines ¼" away from cutting line on both sides. Repeat for all squares.

Positioning Diagram

3. Position and pin squares atop strip set, right sides facing. Align bottom edge of squares with lower edge of strip set and make sure all diagonal lines are angled as shown in *Positioning Diagram*.

4. Stitch on all diagonal sewing lines.

5. Cut around squares.

6. Referring to *Unit Diagrams,* cut each square in half on center diagonal line. Open triangles; press seam allowances toward red and blue triangles. You will have 2 non-matching triangle-squares from each square. Trim each triangle-square to 5½" square.

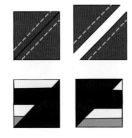

Unit Diagrams

7. Lay out 4 matching triangle-squares as shown in *Block Assembly Diagram.* Join into rows; join rows to complete 1 block *(Red Block Diagram)*.

8. Repeat for navy print units and blue plaid units *(Navy Block Diagram and Blue Block Diagram)*.

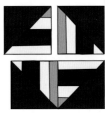

Block Assembly Diagram | Red Block Diagram

Navy Block Diagram | Blue Block Diagram

According to founding father John Adams, Independence Day should be "solemnized with pomp and parade, with shows, games, sports, guns, bells, bonfires, and illuminations, from one end of this continent to the other, from this time forward and forevermore."

Liberty Blocks

Finished size: 2 (10") blocks

MATERIALS
(for 2 blocks)

4 (6") squares red print

40"-long strips assorted gold, red, blue, and cream fabrics in various widths ranging from 1"–2½" wide.

Assembly (makes 2 blocks)

1. Placing wider strips on top and bottom, join assorted strips to make a strip set that measures 6"–6½" from top to bottom as shown in *Strip Set Diagram*. Press seam allowances in one direction.

Strip Set Diagram

2. Draw a cutting line diagonally from corner to corner on wrong side of 1 square. Draw sewing lines ¼" away from cutting line on both sides. Repeat for all squares.

Positioning Diagram

3. Position and pin squares atop strip set, right sides facing. Align bottom edge of squares with lower edge of strip set and make sure all diagonal lines are angled as shown in *Positioning Diagram*.

4. Stitch on all diagonal sewing lines.

5. Cut around squares.

6. Referring to *Unit Diagrams,* cut each square in half on center diagonal line. Open triangles; press seam allowances toward red triangles. Trim each unit to 5½" square.

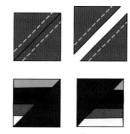

Unit Diagrams

7. Lay out 4 matching units as shown in *Block Assembly Diagram*. Join into rows; join rows to complete 1 block *(Block Diagrams)*. Make 2 blocks.

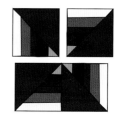

Block Assembly Diagram

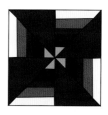

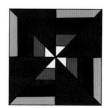

Block Diagrams

With the completion of the Liberty blocks, you can construct Section 4 of your Sampler. See p. 150.

Pursuit of Happiness

Finished size: 1(20") block

Positioning Diagram

Strip Set Diagram

MATERIALS

½ yard navy plaid fabric for star background

1 fat eighth★ red print for star center units

40"-long strips assorted gold, red, blue, and cream fabrics in various widths ranging from 1"–2½" wide.

★fat eighth = 9" × 20"

Cutting

From navy plaid, cut:

• 4 (6") A squares.

• 4 (5½") B squares.

From red print, cut:

• 2 (6") A squares.

Assembly

1. Placing wider strips on top and bottom, join assorted strips to make a strip set that measures 6"–6½" wide from top to bottom as shown in *Strip Set Diagram*. Press seam allowances in one direction.

2. Draw a cutting line diagonally from corner to corner on wrong side of 1 red print A square. Draw sewing lines ¼" away from cutting line on both sides. Repeat for navy plaid A squares and remaining red print A square.

3. Position and pin squares atop strip set, right sides facing. Align bottom edge of squares with lower edge of strip set and make sure all diagonal lines are angled as shown in *Positioning Diagram*.

4. Stitch on all diagonal sewing lines.

5. Cut around squares.

6. Referring to *Unit Diagrams*, cut each square in half on center diagonal line. Open triangles; press seam allowances toward red and navy triangles. Trim each unit to 5½" square.

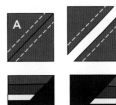

Unit Diagrams

7. Lay out units and navy B squares as shown in *Block Assembly Diagram*. Join into rows; join rows to complete block *(Block Diagram)*.

Block Assembly Diagram

Block Diagram

Blazing Star

Finished size: 1 (12") block

MATERIALS

Fat eighth★ each light gold, dark gold, medium blue, and navy prints

Fat quarter★★ tan print

Lightweight paper for foundations

★Fat eighth = 9" × 20"

★★fat quarter = 18" × 20"

Cutting

From each gold and blue print, cut:
- 2 (4"-wide) strips. From strips, cut 4 (4" × 7½") rectangles.

From tan print, cut:
- 4 (4"-wide) strips. From strips, cut 8 (4" × 7½") rectangles.

Assembly

1. Trace or photocopy 4 each of Foundation Units A and B.

2. Referring to *Sew Easy: Foundation Piecing* on page 27, foundation piece each Unit A in numerical order, using tan print, medium blue print, and dark gold print.

3. Foundation piece each Unit B in numerical order, using tan print, navy print, and light gold print.

4. Trim raw edges even with outer pattern lines.

5. Join 1 Unit A and 1 Unit B to make 1 quadrant as shown in *Block Assembly Diagram*. Make 4 quadrants. Join quadrants to complete block *(Block Diagram)*.

6. Remove paper.

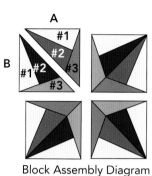

Block Assembly Diagram

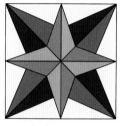

Block Diagram

With the completion of the Blazing Star block, you can construct Section 5 of your Sampler. See p. 151.

In a flash of inspiration, Francis Scott Key wrote the words to our national anthem in 1814. Held aboard a British ship during the bombardment of Baltimore's Ft. McHenry, Key spied the broad stripes and bright, blazing stars of the flag through a haze of gunsmoke. The song, performed in public a few days later, became popular immediately.

Blazing Star Foundation Patterns

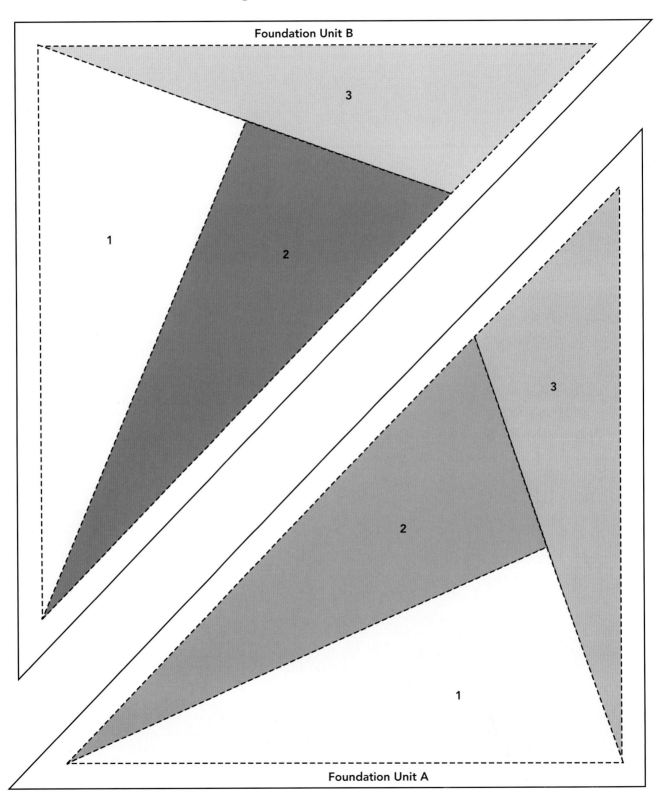

Uncle Sam

Finished size: 1 (10") block

MATERIALS

¼ yard tan print

⅛ yard red print

Scrap (at least 5" × 16") tan and red stripe

Scrap (at least 5" × 9") navy print

1 (3") square medium blue print (E)

Cutting

From tan print, cut:

- 1 (1¾" × 21") strip for strip set.
- 1 (3"-wide) strip. From strip, cut 8 (3" × 1¾") C rectangles.
- 1 (1¾"-wide) strip. From strip, cut 8 (1¾") B squares.

From red print, cut:

- 1 (1¼" × 21") strip for strip set.
- 4 (1¾") squares (D).

From stripe, cut:

- 8 (1¾" × 4¼") A rectangles.

From navy print, cut:

- 8 (1¾") B squares.

Assembly

1. Join 1 tan print and 1 red print strip as shown in *Strip Set Diagram*. Press seam toward red strip. From strip set, cut 8 (1¾"-wide) segments.

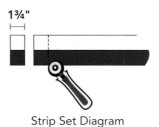

Strip Set Diagram

2. Join 2 segments as shown in *Four Patch Unit Diagrams*. Make 4 Four Patch Units.

Four Patch Unit Diagrams

3. Lay out 2 tan print C rectangles, 1 Four Patch Unit, and 1 red print D square as shown in *Corner Unit Diagrams*. Join to complete 1 Corner Unit. Make 4 Corner Units.

Corner Unit Diagrams

4. Referring to *Diagonal Seams Diagrams,* place 1 tan print B square atop stripe A rectangle. Stitch diagonally from corner to corner. Trim ¼" beyond stitching. Press open to reveal triangle. Repeat for opposite end of rectangle. Make 4 of each unit as shown.

NOTE: Pay careful attention to direction of stitching.

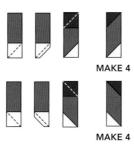

MAKE 4

MAKE 4

Diagonal Seams Diagrams

5. Join 2 stripe units as shown in *Arrow Unit Diagram*. Make 4 Arrow Units.

Arrow Unit Diagram

6. Lay out 4 Corner Units, 4 Arrow Units, and medium blue print E square as shown in *Block Assembly Diagram.*

Block Assembly Diagram

7. Join into rows; join rows to complete block *(Block Diagram).*

Block Diagram

With the completion of the Uncle Sam block, you can construct Section 6 of your Sampler. See p. 151.

Yankee Doodle

Finished size: 1 (10") block

MATERIALS

Fat eighth★ tan print

Scrap (at least 8" × 8") red print #1

Fat eighth★ gold print

Scrap (at least 9" × 12") red print #2

Scrap (at least 4" × 8") navy print

3" square medium blue print (D)

★fat eighth = 9" × 20"

Cutting

From tan print, cut:

• 3 (1¾"-wide) strips. From strips, cut 8 (1¾" × 3") A rectangles and 12 (1¾") B squares.

From red print #1, cut:

• 4 (1¾"-wide) strips. From strips, cut 16 (1¾") B squares.

From red print #2, cut:

• 4 (1¾" × 3") A rectangles.

• 2 (3⅜") squares. Cut squares in half diagonally to make 4 half-square C triangles.

From gold print, cut:

• 2 (3⅜") squares. Cut squares in half diagonally to make 4 half-square C triangles.

• 4 (3") D squares.

From navy print, cut:

• 8 (1¾") B squares.

Assembly

1. Referring to *Flying Geese Unit Diagrams*, place 1 red print #1 B square atop 1 tan print A rectangle, right sides facing. Stitch diagonally from corner to corner. Trim ¼" beyond stitching. Press open to reveal triangle. Repeat for opposite end of rectangle to complete 1 Flying Geese Unit. Make 8 tan Flying Geese Units using red print #1 B squares and tan print A rectangles. Make 4 red Flying Geese Units using tan print B squares and red print #2 A rectangles.

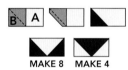

Flying Geese Unit Diagrams

2. Join 1 red print #2 C triangle and 1 gold print C triangle as shown in *Triangle-Square Diagrams*. Make 4 triangle-squares.

Triangle-Square Diagrams

3. Lay out 1 triangle-square, 2 tan Flying Geese Units, and 1 tan print B square as shown in *Corner Unit Diagrams*. Join to complete 1 Corner Unit. Make 4 Corner Units.

Corner Unit Diagrams

4. Referring to *Diagonal Seams Unit Diagrams*, place navy print B square atop gold print D square. Stitch diagonally from corner to corner. Trim ¼" beyond stitching. Press open to reveal triangle. Repeat for adjacent corner to complete 1 Diagonal Seams Unit.

Diagonal Seams Unit Diagrams

4. Join 1 red Flying Geese Unit to 1 Diagonal Seams Unit as shown in *Side Unit Diagrams*. Make 4 Side Units.

Side Unit Diagrams

5. Lay out Corner Units, Side Units, and medium blue print D square as shown in *Block Assembly Diagram*. Join into rows; join rows to complete block (*Block Diagram*).

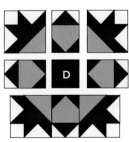
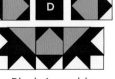
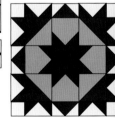

Block Assembly Diagram   Block Diagram

With the completion of the Yankee Doodle block, you can construct Section 7 of your Sampler. See p. 151.

Liberty Star

Finished size: 1 (18") block, including border

MATERIALS

1 (1½" × 40") strip each navy print #1, cream print, and red print for star

Fat quarter★ dark gold print for star background

Fat quarter★ navy print #2 for border

Freezer paper

★fat quarter = 18" × 20"

Cutting

From dark gold print, cut:

• 1 (7¼") square. Cut square in half diagonally in both directions to make 4 quarter-square triangles.

• 4 (4¾") squares.

From navy print #2, cut:

• 2 (2¼" × 15") side border.

• 2 (2¼" × 18½") top and bottom borders.

Assembly

1. Join navy, cream, and red strips, off-setting strips by approximately 1" as shown in *Strip Set Diagram*.

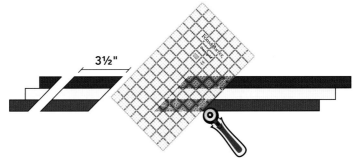

Strip Set Diagram

2. Using 45-degree angle line on ruler as a guide, trim end of strip set at 45-degree angle. To cut a 45-degree diamond, make a second cut *parallel* to the first cut, placing 3½" line on ruler on angled edge. Cut 8 diamonds.

3. Cut 2 (3" × 18") strips from freezer paper. Using 45-degree angle on ruler as a guide, trim end of each paper strip at 45-degree angle line. To cut a 45-degree diamond, make a second cut *parallel* to the first cut, 3" away. Cut 8 paper diamonds. Center and press shiny side of paper diamond to wrong side of fabric diamond to stabilize fabric diamond. Repeat for all diamonds.

4. Lay out 8 diamonds to form a star as shown in *Variation 1 Diagram* or *Variation 2 Diagram*.

Variation 1 Diagram

Variation 2 Diagram

5. Join 4 diamonds to make a half star as shown in *Star Assembly Diagram*. Start and stop stitching at corners of paper diamonds so seam allowances (ends of fabric diamonds) are free, backstitching at beginning and end of seams. Leaving the ends free helps prevent a "lumpy" center and allows for setting triangles and squares into the outside of the star. Repeat to make a second half star. Join star halves as shown in *Star Diagram*.

Star Assembly Diagram

Star Diagram

Star Block Assembly Diagram

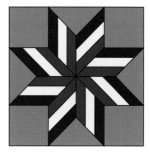

Star Block Diagram

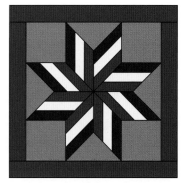

Framed Star Block Diagram

6. Set 1 gold triangle into 1 opening at outside of star as shown in *Star Block Assembly Diagram*. Stitch from outside of star toward the inside, stopping and backstitching ¼" from inner corner (edge of freezer paper). Repeat to join adjacent side of triangle to star. Set 1 triangle into alternate openings around star.

7. In a similar manner, set 1 gold square into each remaining opening to complete block as shown in *Star Block Diagram*. Remove freezer paper backing from diamonds.

8. Add navy print side borders to Star block. Add top and bottom borders to complete framed block (*Framed Star Block Diagram*).

Patriot and orator Patrick Henry spoke his famous words, "Give me liberty or give me death," in 1775, before the Virginia Provincial Convention. As the governor of Virginia, he was the first American politician to call voters "fellow citizens."

Freedom Star Section

Finished size: 1 (18") section
4 (6") Uneven Nine Patch blocks
5 (6") Freedom Star blocks

MATERIALS
(for all blocks)

½ yard tan print
1 fat eighth★ each of navy blue, blue, and brown prints
1 (2" × 20") strip each of five red prints for star points
★fat eighth = 9" × 20"

Cutting (Uneven Nine Patch Blocks)
From tan print, cut:
- 1 (2"-wide) strip. From strip, cut 2 (2" × 20") strips.
- 1 (3½" × 20") strip.

From navy print, cut:
- 1 (3½" × 20") strip.
- 2 (2" × 20") strips.

Uneven Nine Patch Assembly

1. Join 2 (2"-wide) navy print strips and 1 (3½"-wide) tan print strip as shown in *Strip Set 1 Diagram.* Press seams toward navy strips. From strip set, cut 8 (2"-wide) #1 segments.

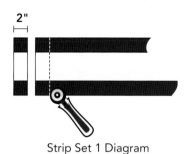

Strip Set 1 Diagram

2. Join 2 (2"-wide) tan strips and 1 (3½"-wide) navy strip as shown in *Strip Set 2 Diagram.* Press seams toward navy strip. From strip set, cut 4 (3½"-wide) #2 segments.

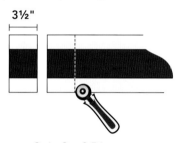

Strip Set 2 Diagram

3. Lay out 2 #1 segments and 1 #2 segment as shown in *Uneven Nine Patch Assembly Diagram.* Join segments to complete 1 Uneven Nine Patch block *(Block Diagram).* Make 4 Uneven Nine Patch blocks.

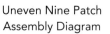

Uneven Nine Patch   Block Diagram
Assembly Diagram

Cutting (Freedom Star Blocks)

From tan print, cut:

- 3 (2"-wide) strips. From strips, cut 20 (2") squares and 20 (2" × 3½") rectangles.

From blue print, cut:

- 2 (2⅜"-wide") strips. From strips, cut 10 (2⅜") squares. Cut squares in half diagonally to make 20 half-square triangles.

From brown print, cut:

- 2 (2⅜"-wide) strips. From strips, cut 10 (2⅜") squares. Cut squares in half diagonally to make 20 half-square triangles.

From each red strip, cut:

- 8 (2") squares.

Star Block Assembly

1. Join 1 blue print triangle and 1 brown print triangle as shown in *Triangle-Square Diagrams.* Make 20 triangle-squares.

Triangle-Square Diagrams

2. Lay out 4 triangle-squares as shown in *Pinwheel Diagrams.* Join into rows; join rows to complete 1 Pinwheel. Make 5 Pinwheels.

Pinwheel Diagrams

3. Referring to *Flying Geese Unit Diagrams,* place 1 red print square atop 1 tan print rectangle, right sides facing. Stitch diagonally from corner to corner. Trim ¼" beyond stitching. Press open to reveal triangle. Repeat for opposite end of rectangle to complete 1 Flying Geese Unit. Make 20 Flying Geese Units.

Flying Geese Unit Diagrams

4. Lay out 1 pinwheel, 4 matching Flying Geese Units, and 4 tan print squares as shown in *Star Block Assembly Diagram.* Join into rows; join rows to complete 1 Star block *(Star Block Diagram).* Make Star 5 blocks.

Star Block Assembly Diagram

Star Block Diagram

5. Lay out blocks as shown in *Freedom Star Section Assembly Diagram.* Join into rows; join rows to complete section *(Freedom Star Section Diagram).*

Freedom Star Section Assembly Diagram

Freedom Star Section Diagram

With the completion of the Freedom Star Section, you can construct Section 8 of your Sampler. See p. 151.

Assembling and Finishing Your Stars & Stripes Sampler

1. Follow instructions on pages 126–149 to make all the blocks for your Stars & Stripes Sampler quilt.

2. Referring to diagrams on this page and page 151, join blocks to make sections.

3. Join sections as shown in *Quilt Center Assembly Diagram* on page 152.

4. From inner border fabric, cut 8 (2"-wide) strips. Piece strips to make 2 (2" × 84½") side inner border strips and 2 (2" × 69½") top and bottom inner border strips.

5. From outer border fabric, cut 9 (6"-wide) strips. Piece strips to make 2 (6" × 87½") side outer border strips and 2 (6" × 80½") top and bottom outer border strips.

6. Add side inner borders to quilt center. Add top and bottom inner borders to quilt. Repeat for outer borders.

7. Divide backing into 3 (2½-yard) lengths. Join panels lengthwise. Seams will run horizontally.

8. Layer backing, batting, and quilt top; baste. Quilt as desired. Quilt shown was machine quilted with varying designs in each block.

9. From binding fabric, cut 10 (2¼"-wide) strips. Join strips into 1 continuous piece for straight-grain French-fold binding. Add binding to quilt.

Section 1

Declaration Star Section American Eagle Vertical Flag

Section 2

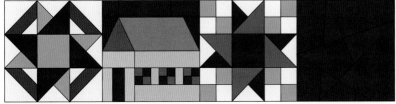

Bunker Hill Star Schoolhouse Lexington Star Lucky Star

Section 3

July 4th Stars

July 4th Stars

Schoolhouse

Little Long Flag

Section 4

Life Horizontal Old Glory Flag Declaration Star Liberty

Section 5

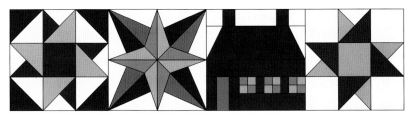

Concord Star   Blazing Star   Schoolhouse   Boston Star

Section 6

Pursuit of Happiness

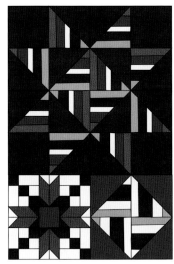

Uncle Sam   Life

Section 7

Life

Yankee Doodle

Liberty

Section 8

Liberty Star

Continental Rose

Horizontal Old Glory Flag

Freedom Star Section

Quilt Center Assembly Diagram

QUILT BY **Shon McMain.**

MACHINE QUILTED BY **Joyce Drexler.**

Wall-size Sampler Quilt

Try this smaller version of our Stars & Stripes Sampler! You'll need only eight blocks.

Finished size: 44" × 50"

MATERIALS

4-6 fat quarters★ cream and tan
  print fabrics
10–12 fat quarters★ assorted red,
  blue, gold, brown, and green
  print, stripe, and plaid fabrics
20½" × 26½" rectangle of cream
  print for eagle background
½ yard navy print for eagle
¼ yard each 1 red and 1 tan print
  for flag stripes
¼ yard navy print for inner border
⅝ yard red print for outer border
½ yard navy print for binding
2¾ yards backing fabric
Crib-size quilt batting
Paper-backed fusible web
★fat quarter = 18" × 20"

Assembly

1. Following instructions on pages
126–146, make 1 horizontal Old
Glory Flag block (Cut C strips 26½"
long and D strips 20½" long for
this quilt),1 Schoolhouse block, 1
Declaration Star block, 1 American
Eagle block, 1 Bunker Hill Star
block, 1 Life block, 1 Blazing Star
block, and 1 Yankee Doodle block.

2. Join blocks to make sections as shown in *Wall-Size Sampler Assembly Diagram*. Join sections to complete quilt center.

3. From inner border fabric, cut 4 (1½"-wide) strips. From strips, cut 2 (1½" × 38½") top and bottom inner borders. Piece strips, if necessary, to make 2 (1½" × 42½") side borders.

4. From outer border fabric, cut 5 (3½"-wide) strips. Join strips to form 1 long strip. Piece strips to make 4 (3½" × 44½") outer borders.

5. Add side inner borders to quilt center. Add top and bottom inner borders to quilt. Repeat for outer borders.

6. Divide backing into 2 (1⅛-yard) lengths. Cut 1 piece in half lengthwise to make 2 narrow panels. Join 1 narrow panel to wider panel. Remaining panel is extra and can be used to make a hanging sleeve.

7. Layer backing, batting, and quilt top; baste.

8. Quilt as desired.

9. From binding fabric, cut 6 (2¼"-wide) strips. Join strips into 1 continuous piece for straight-grain French-fold binding. Add binding to quilt.

Wall-size Sampler Assembly Diagram

Here are two horizontal Wall-size Sampler layouts. Each is 38" × 30" without borders.

Declaration Star Quilt

Iowa quilter Marty Freed combined cozy red, tan, gold, and blue flannels for this masculine quilt.

Finished size: 60" × 80"
18 (10") Declaration Star blocks
17 (10") Four Patch blocks

MATERIALS

5 fat quarters★★ assorted blue plaid, stripe, and check flannels

9 fat quarters★★ assorted red plaid, stripe, and check flannels

9 fat quarters★★ assorted tan plaid, stripe, and check flannels

6 fat eighths★ assorted gold plaid flannels for stars

2⅛ yards navy solid flannel for borders

¾ yard red plaid flannel for binding

5 yards backing fabric

Twin-size quilt batting

Paper-backed fusible web

★fat eighth = 9" × 20"

★★fat quarter = 18" × 20"

Cutting

Measurements include ¼" seam allowances. Border strips are exact length needed. You may want to cut them longer to allow for piecing variations.

Appliqué patterns are on page 130. Follow manufacturer's instructions for using fusible web. To reduce bulk in fusible appliqué, see *Sew Easy: Windowing Fusible Appliqué* on page 13.

From each blue fat quarter, cut:

• 3 (5½"-wide) strips. From strips, cut 8 (5½") squares.

From each red fat quarter, cut:

• 2 (5½"-wide) strips. From strips, cut 4 (5½") squares.

• 2 Circles.

From each tan fat quarter, cut:

• 3 (5½"-wide) strips. From strips, cut 8 (5½") squares.

From each gold fat quarter, cut:

• 3 Stars.

From navy solid, cut:

• 4 (5½"-wide) **lengthwise** strips. From strips, cut 2 (5½" × 70½") side borders and 2 (5½" × 60½") top and bottom borders.

From red plaid, cut:

• 8 (2½"-wide) strips for binding.

Block Assembly

1. Following instructions on page 129, combine pairs of blue and tan squares, red circles, and gold stars to make 18 Declaration Star blocks.

Declaration Star   Four Patch

2. Combine pairs of red and tan squares to make 17 Four Patch blocks.

Note: Marty took liberties with the placement of red, blue, and tan squares, occasionally substituting blue or red plaids in place of tan ones. You can, too, since you will have some extra squares.

Quilt Assembly

1. Referring to photograph on page 155, lay out Declaration Star blocks and Four Patch blocks, alternating blocks as shown.

2. Join blocks into rows; join rows to complete quilt center.

3. Add side borders to quilt center. Add top and botttom borders to quilt.

Finishing

1. Divide backing into 2 (2½-yard) lengths. Cut 1 piece in half length-wise to make 2 narrow panels. Join 1 narrow panel to each side of wider panel. Press seam allowances toward narrow panels.

2. Layer backing, batting, and quilt top; baste.

3. Quilt as desired. Quilt shown was outline quilted around appliqué pieces. Four Patch blocks have Declaration Star motifs quilted on them. Curlicues and stars were stitched in background areas around circles on all blocks. The border has a ribbon and star design.

4. Join 2½"-wide red plaid strips into 1 continuous piece for straight-grain French-fold binding. Add binding to quilt.

Tips for Working with Flannel

• Cut binding strips 2½" wide for flannel.

• Buy extra flannel. Flannels shrink more during pre-washing than cotton broadcloth. Pre-wash flannels and dry in a hot dryer before cutting. Wash darks separately.

• Treat the napped (fuzzy) side of flannel as the fabric right side when cutting and stitching. Spray "wrong" side with spray starch to stiffen fabric before rotary cutting.

• Lengthen your machine stitch length to 8-10 stitches per inch (2.5–3 on European machines) for sewing flannels to reduce stretching and make "unstitching" easier.

• Try utility ("big stitch") quilting with size 8 pearl cotton if you want to hand quilt. Regular quilting thread tends to embed in flannel's loose weave.

QUILT BY **Liz Porter and Marianne Fons.**

MACHINE QUILTED BY **Jean Nolte**.

"Good Morning America" Wall Quilt

When we were asked to be guests on ABC's "Good Morning America" program, we made a quilt just like this, but with the show's title machine embroidered in the center space. The little quilt was hung on a wall at the "Good Morning America" studios in New York City.

Finished size: 32" × 32"
1 (12") Schoolhouse block
4 (10" × 22") horizontal Old Glory
Flag blocks

MATERIALS

for Schoolhouse

1 (1½" × 10") strip each of light gold print and dark gold print for window strip set

1 (2" × 4½") rectangle of brown print for door

1 fat eighth★ navy print for house front and peak

1 fat eighth★ medium blue print for house side

Scrap (at least 5" × 11½") red print for roof

Scrap (at least 6" × 13") cream print for sky

Scrap (at least 3" × 6") dark red print for chimneys

Paper (5" × 13") for foundation

★fat eighth = 9" × 20"

Cutting for Schoolhouse

From navy print, cut:
- 2 (1¾" × 4½") A rectangles.
- 1 (2½" × 4½") B rectangle.
- 1 (5½") square for foundation piecing house peak (F).

From medium blue print, cut:
- 2 (1½" × 2½") C rectangles.
- 2 (2½" × 8½") D rectangles.

From cream print, cut:
- 2 (3½" × 5½") rectangles for foundation piecing (G).

- 2 (2½") J squares.
- 1 (2½" × 5½") H rectangle.

From dark red print, cut:

- 2 (2" × 2½") I chimney rectangles.

MATERIALS

for Flags

Scraps (at least 9" square) of 4 blue
   prints for star fields

Scraps (at least 6" square) of 4 gold
   prints for stars

¼ yard each of 4 red prints for
   stripes

¼ yard each of 4 cream prints for
   stripes

Cutting for Flags

From each blue print, cut:

- 4 (2½") squares.
- 2 (2⅞") squares. Cut squares in half
   diagonally to make 4 half-square
   triangles.

From each gold print, cut:

- 1 (2½") center square.
- 2 (2⅞") squares. Cut squares in half
   diagonally to make 4 half-square
   triangles.

From each red print, cut:

- 2 (2½"-wide) strips. From strips,
   cut 1 (2½" × 22½") C strip and
   2 (2½" × 16½") D strips.

From each cream print, cut:

- 1 (2½"-wide) strip. From strip,
   cut 1 (2½" × 22½") C strip and
   1 (2½" × 16½") D strip.

Quilt Top Assembly Diagram

Block Assembly

1. Following instructions on page
   128, join house pieces to make 1
   Schoolhouse block.
2. Following instructions on page 126,
   join flag pieces to make 4 horizontal
   Old Glory Flag blocks.

Quilt Assembly

1. Lay out flags and Schoolhouse
   block as shown in *Quilt Top Assembly
   Diagram*. Stitch 1 flag to top edge
   of Schoolhouse block with a partial
   seam, stopping at the middle of the
   chimney section.
2. Add flags in clockwise order around
   Schoolhouse.
3. Finish partial seam to complete quilt
   top.

Finishing

MATERIALS

⅜ yard navy print for binding

1 yard backing fabric

Craft-size quilt batting

1. Layer backing, batting, and quilt top;
   baste.
2. Quilt as desired. Quilt shown was
   machine quilted with wavy lines in
   the flag stripes, in the ditch around
   stars and house pieces, and with
   parallel lines on roof piece.
3. From binding fabric, cut 4
   (2¼"-wide) strips. Join strips into 1
   continuous piece for straight-grain
   French-fold binding. Add binding to
   quilt.

QUILT BY **Liz Porter**.
MACHINE QUILTED BY **Kelly Ashton**.

Liz's Lucky Stars Quilt

Liz started playing with free form cutting of shapes, and stumbled upon these Lucky Stars. The technique is a bit tricky, so pay close attention. You'll "thank your Lucky Stars" when you get a pair of blocks that are exact opposites of each other.

Finished size: 71" × 83"

30 (12") Lucky Stars blocks

MATERIALS

30 (13½") squares of assorted plaid, check, and stripe homespun fabrics for stars **NOTE:** Each fabric will form the star in 1 block and the background in the second block.

1 yard each of 3 cream or tan print, stripe, check, or plaid fabrics to outline stars

1⅜ yards of blue stripe homespun for borders

1 yard of red-and-black check for border corners and binding

12½" square ruler (optional)

5 yards of fabric for quilt back

Full-size quilt batting

Cutting

From each cream or tan fabric, cut:

- 25–30 (1"-wide) strips to outline stars.

From blue stripe, cut:

- 7 (6"-wide) strips for borders. Piece strips to make 2 (6" × 72½") side borders and 2 (6" × 60½") top and bottom borders.

From red-and-black check, cut:

- 4 (6") border corner squares.
- 325" of 2½"-wide bias strips. Join strips to make bias binding.

Block Assembly

1. Pair 13½" squares into 15 sets. Make sure the squares contrast well with each other so the star will show up on the background. Each pair of squares will make 2 Lucky Stars blocks.

2. Following instructions on pages 138–139, combine cream strips and pairs of squares to make a total of 30 Lucky Stars blocks.

Quilt Assembly

1. Lay out the blocks as shown in photo on page 159. Join blocks into rows; join rows to complete quilt center.

2. Add blue stripe side borders to quilt center.

3. Join 1 red-and-black check square to each end of top and bottom borders. Add borders to quilt.

Finishing

1. Divide backing fabric into 2 (2½-yard) pieces. Cut one piece in half lengthwise to make 2 narrow panels. Join 1 narrow panel to each side of wider panel. Press seams toward narrow panels.

2. Layer backing, batting, and quilt top; baste.

3. Quilt as desired. Quilt shown was machine quilted in the ditch along cream strips that outline stars and around blocks. Centers of stars are quilted with a Lucky Star shape. Backgrounds of stars and borders are quilted with Lucky Star shapes connected with curly lines.

4. Add binding to quilt.

> ### Sew **Smart**™
>
> When we are using heavier fabric such as flannel or homespun for binding, we like to cut our binding slightly wider (2½" rather than our usual 2¼" width). The added width makes the binding easier to fold over the edges of the somewhat thicker quilt.

> Susan B. Anthony, Quaker-born pioneer in the movement for women's rights, organized the Women's State Temperance Society of New York in 1852. She was president of the National American Woman Suffrage Association from 1892 to 1900. According to quilt historian Carrie Hall, Susan B. Anthony delivered her first talk for the cause of equal rights for women at a quilting bee.

QUILT BY **Liz Porter.**
MACHINE QUILTED BY **Georgia Highley.**

Twisted Sisters Quilt

We call this quilt *Twisted Sisters* because the string-pieced blocks are produced in pairs.
Each "parent" strip set will result in two similar, yet different "sister" blocks.
The blocks twist and turn in pinwheel fashion—twisted sisters!

Finished size: 75½" × 89½"
20 (10") Liberty blocks

MATERIALS

¼ yard each of 10–12 prints or
   stripes in red, blue, gold, tan, and
   cream for strip sets★
3¼ yards dark red print for blocks,
   outer border, and binding
2¼ yards tan check for setting
   pieces
¾ yard blue print for inner border
5½ yards of fabric for quilt back
Full-size quilt batting

★NOTE: Use regular ¼-yard pieces,
not fat quarters, so you can cut
40"-long strips for the strip sets.
After you have cut the setting
pieces and borders from the dark
red, blue, and tan check fabrics,
cut some strips from these to use
in strip sets. Adding even more
fabrics for the strip sets will give
the quilt more character.

Cutting

From each ¼ yard, cut:

- 1 (2"-wide) strip.
- 1 (2½"-wide) strip.
- 1 or 2 (1"-wide) strips.
- 1 or 2 (1½"-wide) strips.

From dark red print, cut:

- 7 (6"-wide) strips. From these, cut 40 (6") squares for blocks.
- 8 (6"-wide) strips for outer borders.
- 9 (2¼"-wide) strips for binding.

From tan check, cut:

- 4 (10½"-wide) strips. From these, cut 12 (10½") setting squares and 2 (8") squares. Cut 8" squares in half diagonally to make 4 corner setting triangles.
- 2 (15½"-wide) strips. From these, cut 4 (15½") squares. Cut squares in half diagonally in both directions to make 16 side setting triangles (2 are extra).

From blue print, cut:

- 8 (2½"-wide) strips for inner border.

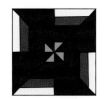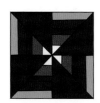

Twisted Sisters Blocks

Liberty Block Assembly

1. Following instructions on page 141, join strips to make a total of 10 strip sets.

2. Make 2 "sister" blocks from each strip set for a total of 20 blocks. Save strip set scraps to make middle pieced border.

Quilt Assembly

1. Referring to photograph on page 161, lay out blocks, setting squares, and setting triangles.

2. Join into diagonal rows; join rows to complete quilt center. If necessary, trim outside edge of quilt top, allowing ¼" seam allowances at corners of blocks.

3. Join pairs of blue print strips to make 4 borders. Measure length of quilt center. Cut side borders to this measurement. Add borders to sides of quilt center. Measure width of quilt center, including side borders. Add borders to top and bottom of quilt.

4. From remainders of strip sets, cut 2½"-wide segments. Measure length and width of quilt top to find border lengths. Join pieced segments to

make 2 borders for quilt sides and 2 for top and bottom edges. From leftover segments, cut 4 (2½") squares for border corners.

5. Stitch pieced borders to sides of quilt. Join 1 border corner to each end of top and bottom borders. Add top and bottom borders to quilt.

6. Join pairs of red border strips to make 4 borders. Measure and trim for side borders; add to quilt. Measure, trim, and add top and bottom borders.

Finishing

1. Divide backing into 2 (2¾-yard) pieces. Cut one piece in half lengthwise to make 2 narrow panels. Join narrow panels to sides of wider panel. Press seams toward narrow panels.

2. Layer backing, batting, and quilt top; baste.

3. Quilt as desired. Quilt shown was machine quilted in the ditch around red triangles and along borders.

4. Join 2¼"-wide dark red print strips into 1 continuous piece for straight-grain French-fold binding. Add binding to quilt.

American Eagle Penny Rug

We used the eagle motif from our sampler quilt for this charming wool table rug. In the nineteenth century, a "rug" was an item to display on a table, bed, or dresser. Floor covering was called "carpet." We blanket stitched our motifs to the background by hand using pearl cotton.

MATERIALS

28½" × 19½" piece of navy wool for background

12" × 25" piece of tan wool for eagle

4" × 10" piece of gold wool for large pennies, stars, and arrows

2 (2" × 28") strips, 2 (2" × 19") strips, and 1 (5" × 5") piece of burgundy wool for borders, shield, and 2 small pennies

3" × 5" piece of teal blue wool for top of shield and 3 small pennies

3" × 3" piece of olive green wool for leaves

Gold and green size 5 pearl cotton

Tracing paper or freezer paper for templates

Cutting & Assembly

1. Using tracing paper or freezer paper and patterns on pages 132–133, trace eagle body, tail, and wing patterns to make templates for eagle. Overlap shapes as indicated. Reverse wing shape to make opposite wing. Make templates for shield pieces, stars, both sizes of pennies, leaf, and arrows.

2. Use templates to cut pieces from fabrics. Trim gold border strips to form sawtooth edging.

Note: If you use freezer paper for your templates, you can lightly press them to your wool to adhere them to the fabric while you are cutting out the pieces. Remove paper after fabric is cut.

3. Referring to photo, position and pin appliqués in place on background rectangle, working from background to foreground. Hand blanket stitch motifs in place. Outline stitch leaf stem *(Blanket Stitch and Outline Stitch Diagrams* on page 133). We used gold thread for all motifs except for the leaves and stem, which were stitched with green.

Sew **Smart**™

Stitch the small pennies to the larger ones before stitching the larger pennies to the background. In the same manner, stitch stars to shield band, and shield and band to eagle body before stitching eagle to background.

General Instructions

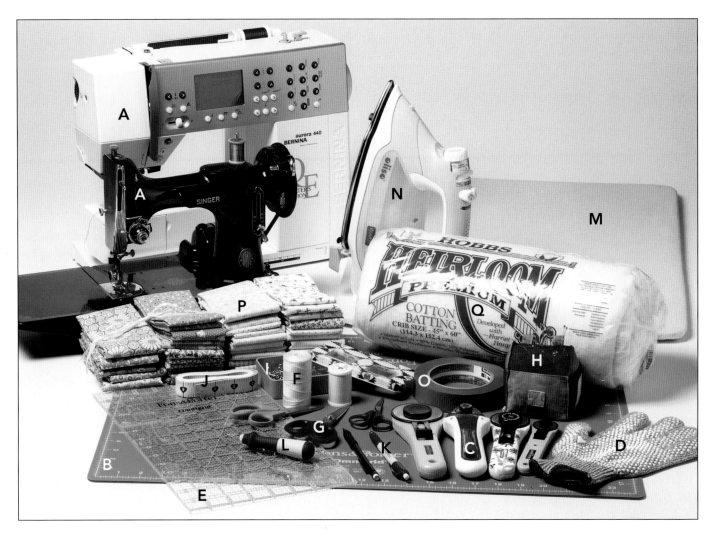

Basic Supplies

You'll need a **sewing machine (A)** in good working order to construct patchwork blocks, join blocks together, add borders, and machine quilt. We encourage you to purchase a machine from a local dealer, who can help you with service in the future, rather than from a discount store. Another option may be to borrow a machine from a friend or family member. If the machine has not been used in a while, have it serviced by a local dealer to make sure it is in good working order. If you need an extension cord, one with a surge protector is a good idea.

A **rotary cutting mat (B)** is essential for accurate and safe rotary cutting. Purchase one that is no smaller than 18" × 24".

Rotary cutting mats are made of "self-healing" material that can be used over and over.

A **rotary cutter (C)** is a cutting tool that looks like a pizza cutter, and has a very sharp blade. We recommend starting with a standard size 45mm rotary cutter. Always lock or close your cutter when it is not in use, and keep it out of the reach of children.

A **safety glove** (also known as a *Klutz Glove)* **(D)** is also recommended. Wear your safety glove on the hand that is holding the ruler in place. Because it is made of cut-resistant material, the safety glove protects your non-cutting hand from accidents that can occur if your cutting hand slips while cutting.

An acrylic **ruler (E)** is used in combination with your cutting mat and rotary cutter. We recommend the Fons & Porter

8" × 14" ruler, but a 6" × 12" ruler is another good option. You'll need a ruler with inch, quarter-inch, and eighth-inch markings that show clearly for ease of measuring. Choose a ruler with 45-degree-angle, 30-degree-angle, and 60-degree-angle lines marked on it as well.

Since you will be using 100% cotton fabric for your quilts, use **cotton or cotton-covered polyester thread (F)** for piecing and quilting. Avoid 100% polyester thread, as it tends to snarl.

Keep a pair of small **scissors (G)** near your sewing machine for cutting threads.

Thin, good quality **straight pins (H)** are preferred by quilters. The pins included with pincushions are normally too thick to use for piecing, so discard them. Purchase a box of nickel-plated brass **safety pins** size #1 **(I)** to use for pin-basting the layers of your quilt together for machine quilting.

Invest in a 120"-long dressmaker's **measuring tape (J)**. This will come in handy when making borders for your quilt.

A 0.7–0.9mm mechanical **pencil (K)** works well for marking on your fabric.

Invest in a quality sharp **seam ripper (L)**. Every quilter gets well-acquainted with her seam ripper!

Set up an **ironing board (M)** and **iron (N)** in your sewing area. Pressing yardage before cutting, and pressing patchwork seams as you go are both essential for quality quiltmaking. Select an iron that has steam capability.

Masking **tape (O)** or painter's tape works well to mark your sewing machine so you can sew an accurate ¼" seam. You will also use tape to hold your backing fabric taut as you prepare your quilt sandwich for machine quilting.

The most exciting item that you will need for quilting is **fabric (P)**. Quilters generally prefer 100% cotton fabrics for their quilts. This fabric is woven from cotton threads, and has a lengthwise and a crosswise grain. The term "bias" is used to describe the diagonal grain of the fabric. If you make a 45-degree angle cut through a square of cotton fabric, the cut edges will be bias edges, which are quite stretchy. As you learn more quiltmaking techniques, you'll learn how bias can work to your advantage or disadvantage.

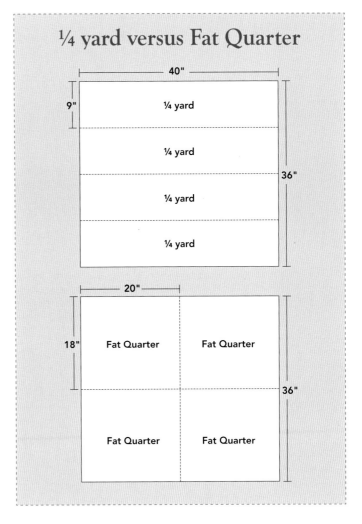

Fabric is sold by the yard at quilt shops and fabric stores. Quilting fabric is generally about 40"–44" wide, so a yard is about 40" wide by 36" long. As you collect fabrics to build your own personal stash, you will buy yards, half yards (about 18" × 40"), quarter yards (about 9" × 40"), as well as other lengths.

Many quilt shops sell "fat quarters," a special cut favored by quilters. A fat quarter is created by cutting a half yard down the fold line into two 18" × 20" pieces (fat quarters) that are sold separately. Quilters like the nearly square shape of the fat quarter because it is more useful than the narrow regular quarter yard cut.

Batting (Q) is the filler between quilt top and backing that makes your quilt a quilt. It can be cotton, polyester, cotton-polyester blend, wool, silk, or other natural materials, such as bamboo or corn. Make sure the batting you buy is at least six inches wider and six inches longer than your quilt top.

Accurate Cutting

Measuring and cutting accuracy are important for successful quilting. Measure at least twice, and cut once!

Cut strips across the fabric width unless directed otherwise.

Cutting for patchwork usually begins with cutting strips, which are then cut into smaller pieces. First, cut straight strips from a fat quarter:

1. Fold fat quarter in half with selvage edge at the top (*Photo A*).

2. Straighten edge of fabric by placing ruler atop fabric, aligning one of the lines on ruler with selvage edge of fabric (*Photo B*). Cut along right edge of ruler.

3. Rotate fabric, and use ruler to measure from cut edge to desired strip width (*Photo C*). Measurements in instructions include ¼" seam allowances.

4. After cutting the required number of strips, cut strips into squares or rectangles as needed.

Setting up Your Sewing Machine

Sew Accurate ¼" Seams

Standard seam width for patchwork and quiltmaking is ¼". Some machines come with a patchwork presser foot, also known as a quarter-inch foot. If your machine doesn't have a quarter-inch foot, you may be able to purchase one from a dealer. Or, you can create a quarter-inch seam guide on your machine using masking tape or painter's tape.

Place an acrylic ruler on your sewing machine bed under the presser foot. Slowly turn handwheel until the tip of the needle barely rests atop the ruler's quarter-inch mark (*Photo A*). Make sure the lines on the ruler are parallel to the lines on the machine throat plate. Place tape on the machine bed along edge of ruler (*Photo B*).

Take a Simple Seam Test

Seam accuracy is critical to machine piecing, so take this simple test once you have your quarter-inch presser foot on your machine or have created a tape guide.

Place 2 (2½") squares right sides together, and sew with a scant ¼" seam. Open squares and finger press seam. To finger press, with right sides facing you, press the seam to one side with your fingernail. Measure across pieces, raw edge to raw edge (*Photo C*). If they measure 4½", you have passed the test! Repeat the test as needed to make sure you can confidently sew a perfect ¼" seam.

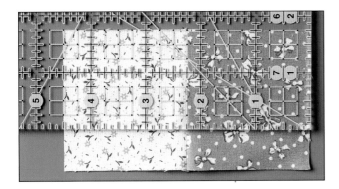

Sewing Comfortably

Other elements that promote pleasant sewing are good lighting, a comfortable chair, background music—and chocolate! Good lighting promotes accurate sewing. The better you can see what you are working on, the better your results. A comfortable chair enables you to sew for longer periods of time. An office chair with a good back rest and adjustable height works well. Music helps keep you relaxed. Chocolate is, for many quilters, simply a necessity.

Tips for Patchwork and Pressing

As you sew more patchwork, you'll develop your own shortcuts and favorite methods. Here are a few favored by many quilters:

● As you join patchwork units to form rows, and join rows to form blocks, press seams in opposite directions from row to row whenever possible (*Photo A*). By pressing seams one direction in the first row and the opposite direction in the next row, you will often create seam allowances that abut when rows are joined (*Photo B*). Abutting or nesting seams are ideal for forming perfectly matched corners on the right side of your quilt blocks and quilt top. Such pressing is not always possible, so don't worry if you end up with seam allowances facing the same direction as you join units.

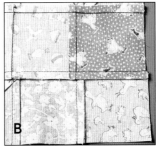

● Sew on and off a small, folded fabric square to prevent bobbin thread from bunching at throat plate (*Photo C*). You'll also save thread, which means fewer stops to wind bobbins, and fewer hanging threads to be snipped. Repeated use of the small piece of fabric gives it lots of thread "legs," so some quilters call it a spider.

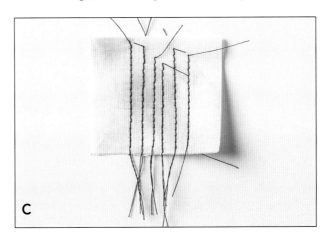

- Chain piece patchwork to reduce the amount of thread you use, and minimize the number and length of threads you need to trim from patchwork. Without cutting threads at the end of a seam, take 3–4 stitches without any fabric under the needle, creating a short thread chain approximately ⅛" long (*Photo D*). Repeat until you have a long line of pieces. Remove chain from machine, clip threads between units, and press seams.

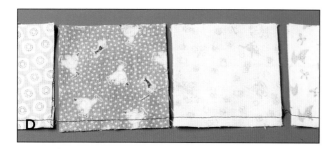

- Trim off tiny triangle tips (sometimes called dog ears) created when making triangle-square units (*Photo E*). Trimming triangles reduces bulk and makes patchwork units and blocks lie flatter. Though no one will see the back of your quilt top once it's quilted, a neat back free of dangling threads and patchwork points is the mark of a good quilter. Also, a smooth, flat quilt top is easier to quilt, whether by hand or machine.

- Careful pressing will make your patchwork neat and crisp, and will help make your finished quilt top lie flat. Ironing and pressing are two different skills. Iron fabric to remove wrinkles using a back and forth, smoothing motion. Press patchwork and quilt blocks by raising and gently lowering the iron atop your work. After sewing a patchwork unit, first press the seam with the unit closed, pressing to set, or embed, the stitching. Setting the seam this way will help produce straight, crisp seams. Open the unit and press on the right side with the seam toward the darkest fabric,

being careful to not form a pleat in your seam, and carefully pressing the patchwork flat.

- Many quilters use finger pressing to open and flatten seams of small units before pressing with an iron. To finger press, open patchwork unit with right side of fabric facing you. Run your fingernail firmly along seam, making sure unit is fully open with no pleat.

- Careful use of steam in your iron will make seams and blocks crisp and flat (*Photo F*). Aggressive ironing can stretch blocks out of shape, and is a common pitfall for new quilters.

Adding Borders

Follow these simple instructions to make borders that fit perfectly on your quilt.

1. Find the length of your quilt by measuring through the quilt center, not along the edges, since the edges may have stretched. Take 3 measurements and average them to determine the length to cut your side borders (*Diagram A*). Cut 2 side borders this length.

2. Fold border strips in half to find center. Pinch to create crease mark or place a pin at center. Fold quilt top in half crosswise to find center of side. Attach side borders to quilt center by pinning them at the ends and the center, and easing in any fullness. If quilt edge is a bit longer than border, pin and sew with border on top; if border is

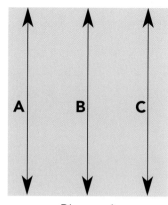

Diagram A

A _____

B _____

C _____

TOTAL _____

_____ ÷3

AVERAGE
LENGTH _____

HELPFUL TIP
Use the following decimal conversions to calculate
your quilt's measurements:

$\frac{1}{8}$" = .125 $\frac{5}{8}$" = .625
$\frac{1}{4}$" = .25 $\frac{3}{4}$" = .75
$\frac{3}{8}$" = .375 $\frac{7}{8}$" = .875
$\frac{1}{2}$" = .5

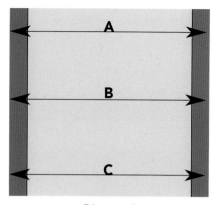

Diagram B

4. Mark centers of borders and top and bottom edges
    of quilt top. Attach top and bottom borders to quilt,
    pinning at ends and center, and easing in any fullness
    (*Diagram C*). Press seams toward borders.

Diagram C

5. Gently steam press entire quilt top on one side and then
    the other. When pressing on wrong side, trim off any
    loose threads.

slightly longer than quilt top, pin and sew with border on
the bottom. Machine feed dogs will ease in the fullness of
the longer piece. Press seams toward borders.

3. Find the width of your quilt by measuring across the
    quilt and side borders (*Diagram B*). Take 3 measurements
    and average them to determine the length to cut your
    top and bottom borders. Cut 2 borders this length.

Joining Border Strips

Not all quilts have borders, but they are a nice complement to a quilt top. If your border is longer than 40", you will need to join 2 or more strips to make a border the required length. You can join border strips with either a straight seam parallel to the ends of the strips (*Photo A*), or with a diagonal seam. For the diagonal seam method, place one border strip perpendicular to another strip, rights sides facing (*Photo B*). Stitch diagonally across strips as shown. Trim seam allowance to ¼". Press seam open (*Photo C*).

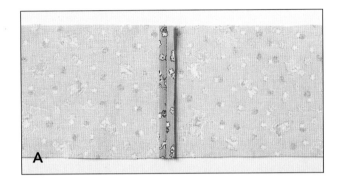

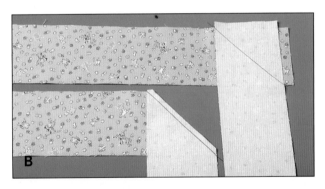

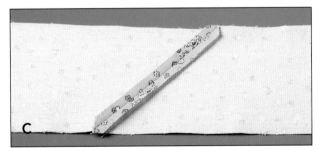

Quilting Your Quilt

Quilters today joke that there are three ways to quilt a quilt—by hand, by machine, or by check. Some enjoy making quilt tops so much, they prefer to hire a professional machine quilter to finish their work. The Split Nine Patch baby quilt shown above has simple machine quilting that you can do yourself.

Decide what color thread will look best on your quilt top before choosing your backing fabric. A thread color that will blend in with the quilt top is a good choice for beginners. Choose backing fabric that will blend with your thread as well. A print fabric is a good choice for hiding less-than-perfect machine quilting. The backing fabric must be at least 3"–4" larger than your quilt top on all 4 sides. For example: if your quilt top measures 44" × 44", your backing needs to be at least 50" × 50". If your quilt top is 80" × 96", then your backing fabric needs to be at least 86" × 102".

For quilt tops 36" wide or less, use a single width of fabric for the backing. Buy enough length to allow adequate margin at quilt edges, as noted above. When your quilt is wider than 36", one option is to use 60"-, 90"-, or 108"-wide fabric for the quilt backing. Because fabric selection is limited for wide fabrics, quilters generally piece the quilt backing from 44/45"-wide fabric. Plan on 40"–42" of usable fabric width when estimating how much fabric to purchase. Plan your piecing strategy to avoid having a seam along the vertical or horizontal center of the quilt.

For a quilt 37"–60" wide, a backing with horizontal seams is usually the most economical use of fabric. For example, for a quilt 50" × 70", vertical seams would require 152", or 4¼ yards, of 44/45"-wide fabric (76" + 76" = 152"). Horizontal seams would require 112", or 3¼ yards (56" + 56" = 112").

Horizontal Seam
Back

Three Panel
Backing

Offset Seam

For a quilt 61"–80" wide, most quilters piece a three-panel backing, with vertical seams, from two lengths of fabric. Cut one of the pieces in half lengthwise, and sew the halves to opposite sides of the wider panel. Press the seams away from the center panel.

For a quilt 81"–120" wide, you will need three lengths of fabric, plus extra margin. For example, for a quilt 108" × 108", purchase at least 342", or 9½ yards, of 44/45"-wide fabric (114" + 114" + 114" = 342").

For a three-panel backing, pin the selvage edge of the center panel to the selvage edge of the side panel, with edges aligned and right sides facing. Machine stitch with a ½" seam. Trim seam allowances to ¼", trimming off the selvages from both panels at once. Press the seam away from the center of the quilt. Repeat on other side of center panel.

For a two-panel backing, join panels in the same manner as above, and press the seam to one side.

Create a "quilt sandwich" by layering your backing, batting, and quilt top. Find the crosswise center of the backing fabric by folding it in half. Mark with a pin on each side. Lay backing down on a table or floor, wrong side up. Tape corners and edges of backing to the surface with masking or painter's tape so that backing is taut (*Photo A*).

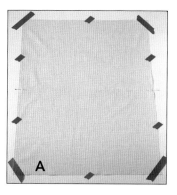

Fold batting in half crosswise and position it atop backing fabric, centering folded edge at center of backing (*Photo B*). Unfold batting and smooth it out atop backing (*Photo C*).

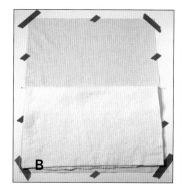
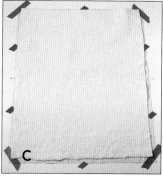

In the same manner, fold the quilt top in half crosswise and center it atop backing and batting (*Photo D*). Unfold top and smooth it out atop batting (*Photo E*).

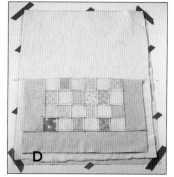

Use safety pins to pin baste the layers (*Photo F*). Pins should be about a fist width apart. A special tool, called a Kwik Klip, or a grapefruit spoon makes closing the pins easier. As you slide a pin through all three layers, slide the point of the pin into one of the tool's grooves. Push on the tool to help close the pin.

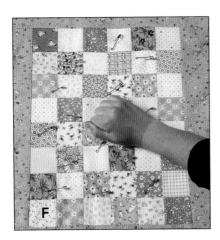

For straight line quilting, install an even feed or walking foot on your machine. This presser foot helps all three layers of your quilt move through the machine evenly without bunching.

Walking Foot   Stitching "in the ditch"

An easy way to quilt your first quilt is to stitch "in the ditch" along seam lines. No marking is needed for this type of quilting.

Binding Your Quilt

Preparing Binding

Strips for quilt binding may be cut either on the straight of grain or on the bias. For the quilts in this booklet, cut strips on the straight of grain.

1. Measure the perimeter of your quilt and add approximately 24" to allow for mitered corners and finished ends.
2. Cut the number of strips necessary to achieve desired length. We like to cut binding strips 2¼" wide.
3. Join your strips with diagonal seams into 1 continuous piece (*Photo A*). Press the seams open. (See page 170 for instructions for the diagonal seams method of joining strips.)

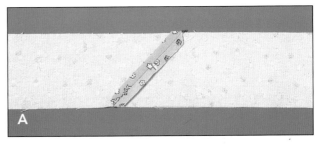

4. Press your binding in half lengthwise, with wrong sides facing, to make French-fold binding (*Photo B*).

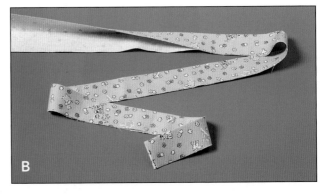

Attaching Binding

Attach the binding to your quilt using an even-feed or walking foot. This prevents puckering when sewing through the three layers.

1. Choose beginning point along one side of quilt. Do not start at a corner. Match the two raw edges of the binding strip to the raw edge of the quilt top. The folded edge

will be free and to left of seam line (*Photo C*). Leave 12" or longer tail of binding strip dangling free from beginning point. Stitch, using ¼" seam, through all layers.

2. For mitered corners, stop stitching ¼" from corner; backstitch, and remove quilt from sewing machine (*Photo D*). Place a pin ¼" from corner to mark where you will stop stitching.

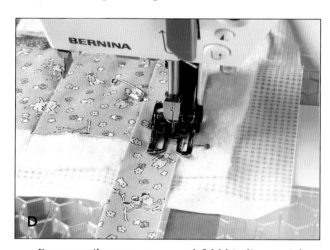

Rotate quilt quarter turn and fold binding straight up, away from corner, forming 45-degree-angle fold (*Photo E*).

Bring binding straight down in line with next edge to be sewn, leaving top fold even with raw edge of previously sewn side (*Photo F*). Begin stitching at top edge, sewing through all layers (*Photo G*).

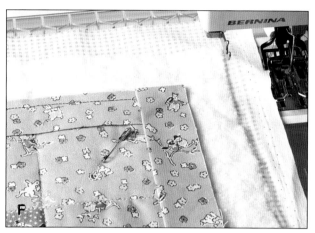

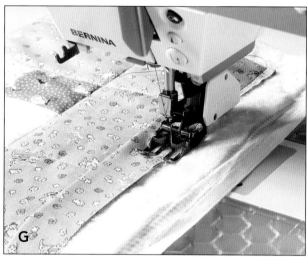

3. To finish binding, stop stitching about 8" away from starting point, leaving about a 12" tail at end (*Photo H*). Bring beginning and end of binding to center of 8" opening and fold each back, leaving about ¼" space

between the two folds of binding (*Photo I*). (Allowing this ¼" extra space is critical, as binding tends to stretch when it is stitched to the quilt. If the folded ends meet at this point, your binding will be too long for the space after the ends are joined.) Crease folds of binding with your fingernail.

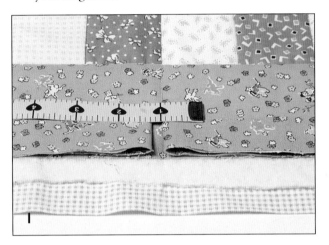

4. Open out each edge of binding and draw line across wrong side of binding on creased fold line, as shown in *Photo J*. Draw line along lengthwise fold of binding at same spot to create an X (*Photo K*).

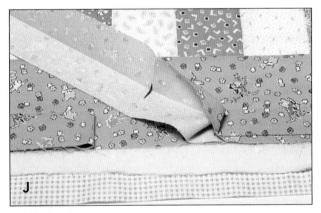

5. With edge of ruler at marked X, line up 45-degree-angle marking on ruler with one long side of binding (*Photo L*). Draw diagonal line across binding as shown in *Photo M*.

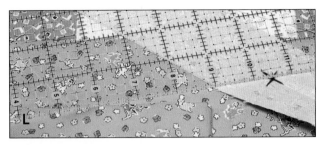

Repeat for other end of binding. Lines must angle in same direction (*Photo N*).

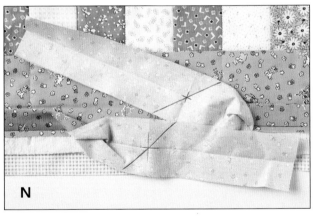

6. Pin binding ends together with right sides facing, pin-matching diagonal lines as shown in *Photo O*. Binding ends will be at right angles to each other. Machine-stitch along diagonal line, removing pins as you stitch (*Photo P*).

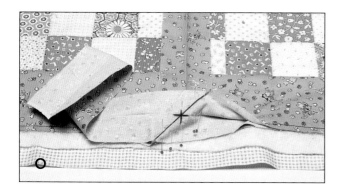

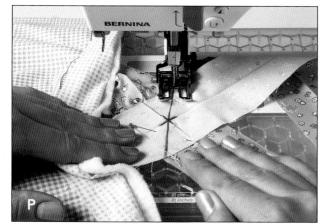

7. Lay binding against quilt to double-check that it is correct length (*Photo Q*). Trim ends of binding ¼" from diagonal seam (*Photo R*).

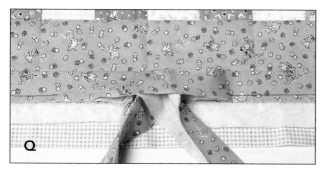

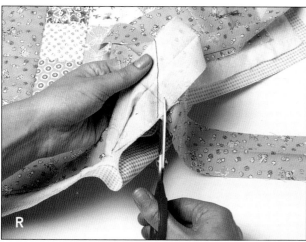

8. Finger press diagonal seam open (*Photo S*). Fold binding in half and finish stitching binding to quilt (*Photo T*).

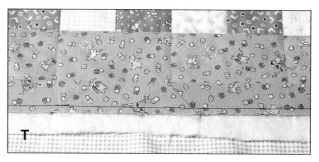

Hand Stitching Binding to Quilt Back

1. Trim any excess batting and quilt back with scissors or a rotary cutter (*Photo A*). Leave enough batting (about ⅛" beyond quilt top) to fill binding uniformly when it is turned to quilt back.

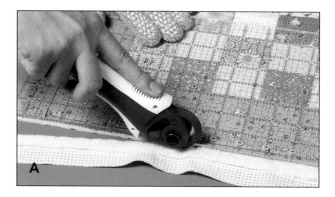

2. Bring folded edge of binding to quilt back so that it covers machine stitching. Blindstitch folded edge to quilt backing, using a few pins just ahead of stitching to hold binding in place (*Photo B*).

3. Continue stitching to corner. Fold unstitched binding from next side under, forming a 45-degree angle and a mitered corner. Stitch mitered folds on both front and back (*Photo C*).

Finishing Touches

- **Label your quilt so the recipient and future generations know who made it.** To make a label, use a fabric marking pen to write the details on a small piece of solid color fabric (*Photo A*). To make writing easier, put pieces of masking tape on the wrong side. Remove tape after writing. Use your iron to turn under ¼" on each edge, then stitch the label to the back of your quilt using a blindstitch, taking care not to sew through to quilt top.

- **Take a photo of your quilt.** Keep your photos in an album or journal along with notes, fabric swatches, and other information about the quilts.

- **If your quilt is a gift, include care instructions.** Some quilt shops carry pre-printed care labels you can sew onto the quilt (*Photo B*). Or, make a care label using the method described above.

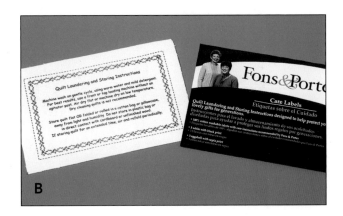